THE BRITISH FILM GUIDES

The celebrated film director François Truffaut once famously observed that there was a certain incompatibility between the terms British and cinema. That was typical of the critical disparagement for so long suffered by British films. As late as 1969 a respected film scholar could dub British cinema 'the unknown cinema'. This was the situation because up to that time the critics, scholars and intellectuals writing about cinema preferred either continental films or latterly Hollywood to the homegrown product. Over the past thirty years that position has changed dramatically. There are now monographs, journals, book series, university courses and conferences entirely devoted to British cinema.

The Tauris British Film Guide series seeks to add to that process of revaluation by assessing in depth key British films from the past hundred years. Each film guide will establish the historical and cinematic context of the film, provide a detailed critical reading and assess the reception and after-life of the production. The series will draw on all genres and all eras and will over time build into a wide-ranging library of informed, in-depth books on the films that have defined British cinema. It is a publishing project that will comprehensively refute Truffaut's ill-informed judgement and demonstrate the variety, creativity, humanity, poetry and mythic power of the best of British cinema.

JEFFREY RICHARDS
General Editor, the British Film Guides

British Film Guides published and forthcoming:

The Charge of the Light Brigade Mark Connelly
The Dam Busters John Ramsden
Dracula Peter Hutchings
My Beautiful Laundrette Christine Geraghty
A Night to Remember Jeffrey Richards
The Private Life of Henry VIII Greg Walker
The Red Shoes Mark Connelly
The 39 Steps Mark Glancy
Whisky Galore! and The Maggie Colin McArthur

A BRITISH FILM GUIDE

Whisky Galore! and The Maggie

COLIN McARTHUR

I.B. TAURIS

LONDON · NEW YORK

Published in 2003 by I.B. Tauris & Co Ltd
6 Salem Road, London W2 4BU
175 Fifth Avenue, New York NY 10010
www.ibtauris.com

In the United States of America and Canada distributed by Palgrave
Macmillan a division of St Martin's Press, 175 Fifth Avenue, New York
NY 10010

ISBN 1 86064 633 6

A full CIP record for this book is available from the British Library
A full CIP record for this book is available from the Library of Congress

Library of Congress catalog card: available

Set in Monotype Fournier and Univers Black by Ewan Smith, London
Printed and bound in Great Britain by MPG Books, Bodmin

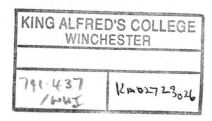

Contents

Illustrations / vi
Acknowledgements / vii

Film Credits   1

Introduction: The Critical Question   3

1   The Moment(s) of *Whisky Galore!* and *The Maggie*   7

2   Inside *Whisky Galore!* and *The Maggie*   34

3   Post-production: Marketing and Consuming   81

Notes   101
Sources   103

Illustrations

1. Mackenzie's novel marketed within the 'iconography of popular Scottishness'.   17

2. A clash of cultures: American tycoon; Scottish puffer.   29

3. George Campbell (Gordon Jackson) confronted by his mother (Jean Cadell). The bagpiping patriarch is on the wall behind her.   40

4. Alexander Mackendrick rehearses the 'chaste' love scene with Joan Greenwood and Bruce Seton.   42

5. A calculating look in her eye. Joan Greenwood as Peggy Macroon.   43

6. The three myths of whisky …

   a) … whisky as healthgiving. Doctor Maclaren (James Robertson Justice) rejuvenates old Hector.   48

   b) … whisky as adjunct to sociability. The 'mouth music' scene.   48

   c) … whisky as generator of masculinity. Doctor Maclaren gives George the dram that will allow him to face his mother.   49

7. Communitarian framing. The crew of *The Maggie*, from left to right, Douggie (Tommy Kearins), Mactaggart (Alex Mackenzie), the Engineman (Abe Barker) and the Mate (James Copeland).   57

8. 'Like a penitent in a religious ceremony': the humiliation of Marshall.   70

9. Marshall (Paul Douglas) is led into the dance by 'the Spirit of Scotland' (Fiona Clyne).   72

10. The individual versus the community. Marshall and the crew in the final confrontation.   79

11. This montage from a German publicity leaflet not only shows a stunned Waggett (Basil Radford) bottom left, but also George Campbell (Gordon Jackson), bottom right after he has played his mother into silence and, top right, having his courage wound up by Doctor Maclaren (James Robertson Justice) so that he can face her.   82

Acknowledgements

It was Jeffrey Richards's idea to include in this book both *Whisky Galore!* and *The Maggie* rather than (my original intention) just the latter. I think the book has benefited from this and from Jeffrey's helpful suggestions during his sympathetic editing. Philip Kemp was generous both with his time and papers, giving me access to various documents relating to Mackendrick, including yet unpublished interviews. David Meeker and Heather Osborne of the BFI, and Steve Jenkins and Alice Bruggen of the BBC, supplied data about the historical visibility of both films on cinema and television screens, and Michael Søby and Johan Hage of the Royal Danish Embassy in London supplied translations of Danish reviews of *Whisky Galore!* The staff of the BFI Library serviced my every need and Janet Moat of BFI Special Collections dug out relevant documents deeply buried in the Balcon and Montagu papers. I had useful conversations about theoretical issues, the films themselves and/or Scottish (film) culture with John Brown, Murray Grigor, Frederic Lindsay, Colin Macleod, Finlay Macleod, Lindsay Paterson and Mike Wayne. As always, the labour of my wife Tara is also in this book. More than anyone, it is she who keeps this old crock on the road and maintains the optimism necessary to go on.

Stills appear here by courtesy of Canal Plus. They are reproduced here for the purposes of critical analysis.

For my children – Elena, Marni and Ravi

Film Credits

WHISKY GALORE! (US: *TIGHT LITTLE ISLAND*)

Production Company	Ealing Studios
Producer	Michael Balcon
Associate Producer	Monja Danischewsky
Director	Alexander Mackendrick
Screenplay	Compton Mackenzie and Angus MacPhail (based on Mackenzie's novel of the same name)
Cinematographer	Gerald Gibbs
Editor	Joseph Sterling
Music	Ernest Irving
Music Director	Ernest Irving with the Philharmonia Orchestra
Art Director	Jim Morahan
Sound Supervisor	Stephen Dalby
Production Supervisor	Hal Mason
Assistant Director	Harry Kratz
Camera Operator	Chick Waterson
Sound Recordist	Leonard B. Bulkley
Wardrobe Supervisor	Anthony Mendleson
Continuity	Marjorie Owens
Special Effects	Geoffrey Dickinson and Sydney Pearson
Unit Production Manager	L. C. Rudkin
Running time	82 minutes (7,457 feet)
UK Première	16 June 1949
US Première	19 December 1949

CAST

The English: Basil Radford (Captain Paul Waggett), Catherine Lacey (Mrs Waggett), Bruce Seton (Sergeant Odd).

The Islanders: Joan Greenwood (Peggy Macroon), Wylie Watson (Joseph Macroon), Gabrielle Blunt (Catriona Macroon), Gordon Jackson (George Campbell), Jean Cadell (Mrs Campbell), James Robertson Justice (Doctor Maclaren), Morland Graham (The Biffer), John Gregson (Sammy MacCodrum), James Woodburn (Roderick MacRurie), James Anderson (Old Hector), Jameson Clark (Constable Macrae), Duncan Macrae (Angus MacCormac), Mary MacNeil (Mrs MacCormac), Norman MacOwan (Captain MacPhee), Alastair Hunter (Captain MacKechnie).

The Others: Henry Mollison (Mr Farquarson), Frank Webster (First Mate), Compton Mackenzie (Captain Buncher), Finlay Currie (Narrator).

THE MAGGIE (US: *HIGH AND DRY*)

Production Company	Ealing Studios
Producer	Michael Truman
Director	Alexander Mackendrick
Screenplay	William Rose
Original Story	Alexander Mackendrick
Cinematographer	Gordon Dines
Editor	Peter Tanner
Music	John Addison
Conducted by	Dock Mathieson with the Philharmonia Orchestra
Art Director	Jim Morahan
Costume Supervisor	Anthony Mendleson
Sound Supervisor	Stephen Dalby
Production Supervisor	Hal Mason
Assistant Director	Frank Gollings
Camera Operators	Chick Waterson and Hugh Wilson
Sound Recordist	Leo Wilkins
Special Processes	Geoffrey Dickinson
Special Effects	Sydney Pearson
Make-up	Alex Garfath
Continuity	Barbara Cole
Unit Production Manager	L.C. Rudkin
Running time	92 minutes (8,330 feet)
UK Première	25 February 1954
US Première	1 September 1954

CAST

Paul Douglas (Calvin B. Marshall), Alex Mackenzie (Captain Mactaggart), James Copeland (The Mate), Abe Barker (The Engineman), Tommy Kearins (The Wee Boy), Hubert Gregg (Pusey), Geoffrey Keen (Campbell), Dorothy Alison (Miss Peters), Andrew Keir (The Reporter), Meg Buchanan (Sarah), Mark Dignam (The Laird), Jameson Clark (Dirty Dan), Moultrie Kelsall (CSS Skipper), Fiona Clyne (Sheena), Sheila Shand Gibbs (Barmaid), Betty Henderson (Campbell's Secretary), Russell Waters and Duncan Macintyre (Hailing Officers), Roddy Macmillan (Inverkerran Driver), Jack Macguire (Highland Innkeeper), John Rae (The Constable), Jack Stewart and Eric Woodburn (Skippers), Douglas Robin and R. B. Wharrie (Inspectors), David Cameron (Hired Car Driver), Catherine Fletcher (Postmistress), William Crichton (Harbour Master), Andrew Downie (Aircraft Pilot), Herbert C. Cameron (Gillie), Gilbert Stevenson (Davy MacDougall).

Introduction: The Critical Question

No act of (film) criticism is innocent. Whether or not the critic is aware of it, a critical project is always being enacted. The immediate context of this book is a series entitled British Film Guides, the aim of each being to tell 'the full story of an important British film'. Unusually, this volume is about *two* films: *Whisky Galore!* and *The Maggie*. They have at least three important things in common: both are productions of Ealing Studios; both are directed by Alexander Mackendrick; and both offer representations of Scotland and the Scots. While this book will honour the aim of the series, without question it is the third of these that most animates the writer and has driven him to write the book. As it happens, the dominant critical paradigms within which these films have been discussed (or, perhaps better, *constructed*) relate to the other two, most cogently exemplified by Charles Barr's *Ealing Studios* and Philip Kemp's *Lethal Innocence: the Cinema of Alexander Mackendrick*, the former primarily concerned to locate the films as British (actually *English*), the latter as films substantially shaped by Mackendrick's dark and complex sensibility. The present writer referred to both films in passing in an essay entitled 'Scotland and Cinema: the Iniquity of the Fathers' in a book called *Scotch Reels: Scotland in Cinema and Television*. This volume offers the opportunity not only of a more in-depth account of these films, but also of demonstrating that what the other paradigms tend to see as a 'natural' and 'realistic' representation of Scotland and the Scots is, in fact, highly ideological. A recent discussion of *Whisky Galore!* and *The Maggie*, more homologous with that of *Scotch Reels*, occurs in Christine Geraghty's *British Cinema of the Fifties: Gender, Genre and the 'New Look'*. Geraghty locates the films in a wider frame-work than *Scotch Reels*, seeing them – along with other British filmic representations of rural Ireland and England of the time – as simply one cultural site within which the British talked to themselves about the problems of (primarily post-war) modernity.

Scotch Reels has recently been critiqued in three separate works: Pam Cook's *Fashioning the Nation: Costume and Identity in British Cinema*, Jeffrey Richards's *Film and British National Identity: from Dickens to Dad's Army*, and Duncan Petrie's *Screening Scotland*. Their diverse arguments need more detailed consideration than is possible here but, at the risk of simplifying and homogenizing their positions, all three share certain tendencies about which I am sceptical. Broadly speaking, they are all populist works, in the sense not only of dealing primarily with popular cinema, but of according it higher levels of excellence than I believe to be consistently warranted; a feeling that because many people like it, it is somehow always on the side of the angels. Built into this position (particularly Cook's version of it) is the idea that popular films are complex artefacts that may be critical of the ideologies they are themselves founded on, either at an unconscious level (Cook) or as a result of the purposive activity of their makers (Petrie). This tendency to be (almost) wholly up-beat about popular cinema – one of the major criticisms of *Scotch Reels* was its alleged disdain for movies that people like – becomes tangled up with a distancing from the knowledge gained from the theoretical debates of the 1970s and a drift away from some of the categories which circulated in these debates, particularly *class* and *ideology*. Taken together, these tendencies seem to me to leave a danger-ous lacuna in the critical lexicon, particularly in the current climate in which, increasingly, films that do not conform to a very narrow range of popular genres are pushed further and further to the margins and the historical memory of the diversity of cinema becomes yearly more atrophied. It is all very well demonstrating and celebrating 'the com-plexity of the popular', but responsible film criticism must also be alert to the regressive aspects of the popular. *Braveheart* is the most notorious recent example, a film which, to his credit, Jeffrey Richards denounces, but in somewhat problematic terms which stress the film's historical inaccuracies rather than the ideological reasons for them. A responsible criticism must also be committed to retaining in the public memory those films which offer alternative ways of making cinema, but that is an argument which must be conducted elsewhere than in these pages.[1]

To some extent *Scotch Reels* was misread. Because it mounted a trenchant ideological critique of the way Scotland and the Scots have been represented on screen, it was widely assumed that its writers found films such as *Whisky Galore!* and *The Maggie* worthless. As I hope the following pages will demonstrate, this was not the case. Indeed, an important aim of this book is to retrieve *The Maggie* in particular from the critical Sargasso Sea into which it has all but vanished. What the book does, therefore, is to apply what Terry Eagleton calls a 'redemptive hermeneutic'.[2] That is, it engages with two films, certain ideological aspects of which I find troubling, not simply to expose their ideological workings but to point to elements in them which are constructive, pleasurable and worthy of attention. Aspects of the practice of this method have something in common with that of the French literary theorist Pierre Macherey for whom 'a work is tied to ideology not so much by what it says as by what it does not say. It is in the significant *silences* of a text, in its gaps and absences that the presence of ideology can be most positively felt. It is these silences which the critic must make "speak".'[3]

Part of the difficulty of critiquing the 'complexity of the popular' position is that this book's critical method overlaps with aspects of it, accepting that the popular (and, perhaps more importantly, the ways in which the popular is read and used) may indeed be complex. However, my attempt to hold together what I will call the 'conscious' and the 'unconscious' elements of *Whisky Galore!* and *The Maggie* and my wish visibly to retain the concept of *class* as well as those of *gender* and *ethnicity* in the critical lexicon, sets my method somewhat apart. I am aware that the class/gender/ethnicity triptych has been something of a mantra on the left as a way of trying to explain the most common forms of oppression and that it contains a raft of complex theoretical problems regarding the status of each part of the triptych. For example, gender and ethnicity are written irredeemably on our bodies (*pace* Dana International and Michael Jackson) in a way that class is not. Partly for this reason – and very much under the sign of Foucault – there is an increasing tendency to stress gender and ethnicity at the expense of class. This is a tendency I would wish to resist, partly for political reasons (no one familiar with, for example, the recent debate about Oxbridge selection could doubt the continuing explanatory power of the concept of class) and partly for aesthetic/ideological reasons – the silences of *Whisky Galore!* and *The Maggie* relate to class as well as to gender and ethnicity.

Alan Lovell entitled a recent essay 'British Cinema: the Known Cinema', a reference to his own 1969 paper 'British Cinema: the Unknown Cinema' and formulated specifically to highlight the extent to which British cinema has gone from being a virtual *terra incognita* to becoming of central critical interest within British (and to some extent American and Australian) film studies over the intervening three decades.

In this context, Charles Barr's book on Ealing Studios looks in retrospect like one of the opening moves in the long process of anatomizing and classifying British cinema, an ongoing process of which this book and the series in which it appears are part. There are many voices clamouring to be heard in this rethinking, so it is particularly important that every contribution be seen not simply as adding to the sum of knowledge of the subject. Questions need to be asked about the critical projects implicit within these diverse voices, judgements made about the relative import-ance of the critical issues being raised. For critical projects may not simply be lying side by side, each contributing a different 'truth' about the subject. To raise one set of questions may involve repressing others or simply not recognizing that they exist as legitimate questions. This volume argues that such has been the case with regard to *Whisky Galore!* and *The Maggie*.

ONE
The Moment(s) of *Whisky Galore!* and *The Maggie*

[Mackenzie theorized] that nations had a sex – England, Germany
and Spain were masculine, Scotland, Greece and France were
feminine.[1]

It is often said that every film reflects the moment of its production,
telling us much about the society out of which it comes. There is an
obvious sense in which this is true. *Whisky Galore!* appeared in 1949 in
the middle of what has been called 'austerity Britain', that half-dozen
years of the two post-war Labour governments in which rationing
continued, consumer goods were in short supply and the darkness of the
wartime blackout seemed to hang metaphorically over the land. It is
tempting to see *Whisky Galore!*, with its bonanza of innumerable cases
of whisky being deposited off a whisky-starved Scottish island, as a
potent utopian fantasy generated by the social conditions of the time.
Indeed, the publisher's blurb for the 1961 Penguin reprint of the novel
described it as 'non-austerity in every respect'. *The Maggie*, on the other
hand, appeared in 1953 when a rather different set of socio-economic
conditions prevailed. Although not quite the boom period of Harold
Macmillan's 1957 Conservative government, with its slogan 'You've
never had it so good', the early 1950s had something of the semblance
of an emergence from austerity. To some extent the incoming Tory
administration benefited from the Labour government's attempt to re-
orient the national mood towards greater optimism with the Festival of
Britain – that 'tonic to the nation' which was already making itself felt
in a brighter design environment – and, despite the underlying structural
problem of Britain's relative economic decline, a short-term reversal of
the national balance of payments deficit contributed to the popular
perception that Britain was finally leaving behind the dark days of the
1940s. However, one of the undersides of this apparent boom was the

escalating intrusion of American capital into Britain, not least to Scotland, the clashing mores generated by which are discernible in *The Maggie*. So, adding the two dominant critical paradigms referred to in the Introduction – those relating to Ealing Studios and to Alexander Mackendrick – there might be a tendency to read *Whisky Galore!* solely in terms of the moment of 1949 and to discuss it in terms of the social background of the time, what was happening concurrently in Ealing Studios, and what emerged from Mackendrick's debut as a film director. Such an approach might be rendered diagrammatically as:

1949

First Labour government – austerity

Ealing Studios – move to location shooting

Mackendrick – directorial debut

A similar 'cross-section' model for *The Maggie* might be represented as:

1953

Tory government/emerging affluence/US capital

Ealing Studios – perceived to be in decline

Mackendrick – mature and experienced

While much useful knowledge about both films might be gleaned from such an approach, what it leaves out of account are the long-term, unconscious discourses shaping both films and which were in place and active long before 1949 and 1953. The most important of these relate to gender, class and ethnicity. The unconscious discourse relating to gender is usually called patriarchal; the unconscious discourse relating to class emerges from the dominance – in the modern world certainly up to the 1940s and the 1950s – of middle-class perceptions of the world; and the unconscious discourse relating to ethnicity, in the context of *Whisky Galore!* and *The Maggie* , is that which constructs the Scots (in particular the Gaelic-speaking, Highland Scots) as having an essential identity different from – indeed, in many respects the antithesis of – the Anglo-Saxon identity exemplified by (a certain class of) Englishmen and Americans. That ethnic discourse will be referred to in these pages as the Scottish Discursive Unconscious. There is an added complication with regard to *Whisky Galore!* Intertwined with and mapped over these three unconscious discourses is the strange and powerful sensibility of Compton Mackenzie, writer of the original novel on which *Whisky Galore!* was based and contributor to the screenplay itself. No such powerful sensibility obtrudes upon the development of *The Maggie*, although that of the screenwriter William Rose was not insignificant. It is this mixture of the contemporary and the historical which makes it appropriate to speak of the moment(s) of the films, for they can be discussed both in relation to their specific times of 1949 and 1953 and to the longer historical moment of which they are both part. Represented diagrammatically, this latter way of reading the films would look like this:

1949	1953
Whisky Galore!	*The Maggie*
Labour/austerity	Tory/affluence
Ealing rising	Ealing in decline
Mackendrick emerging	Mackendrick mature
the Mackenzie discourse	
	the William Rose discourse

.... the class discourse ....
.. the gender discourse ....
.... the Scottish Discursive Unconscious ....

With both films the meaning is not derived solely from their years of production; arguably more important are the deeply sedimented meanings which pass into the films unconsciously through the discourses within which the personnel making the films were born and raised and which they would have regarded as natural; to use Althusser's term, the discourses within which they were *interpellated*. It is part of the argument of this book that this kind of reading, which might be called a differential temporalities reading, prising as it does the films out of their own specific time and seeing them as shaped by impulses from diverse historical moments, offers a more complex account of the films, telling 'the full story' as the series intends. It should be added that attempts to render, by way of diagram or metaphor, the way discursivity operates, in no way do justice to the complexity, fluidity and leakiness of discourse(s). One has recourse simply to additional metaphors such as Chinese boxes and Russian dolls, images which attempt to convey the overlap element, the palimpsest quality, of diverse discourses. Concretely, it would have been possible to add, as another layer to the above diagram, the deeply sedimented discourse of modernity. Christine Geraghty (in the book mentioned in the Introduction) deploys this discourse to illuminate British films of the 1950s, including *Whisky Galore!* and, more particularly, *The Maggie*, enveloping what I have called the Scottish Discursive Unconscious within the wider discourse of modernity.

Both the conscious and the unconscious shaping of the films came about primarily from the inputs of the key creative personnel who worked on them, defined here as those involved in the choice of subjects and the writing and directing of them. These are, in the case of *Whisky Galore!*, novelist and co-screenwriter Compton Mackenzie (1883–1972), producer Michael Balcon (1896–1977), associate producer Monja Danischewsky (1911–94), co-screenwriter Angus MacPhail (1903–62), and director Alexander Mackendrick (1912–93); and in the case of *The Maggie*, Balcon and Mackendrick again plus screenwriter William Rose (1918–87) and producer Michael Truman (1916–72). To call them the key creative personnel is not to impugn the roles of the actors, cinematographers, set designers, musical directors and others, simply to underline that the contributions of the latter are almost invariably subject to the will of the former. The argument is that by the nature of the period in which they were formed as social beings, these men – and the fact that there are no women among them is part of the argument – would have been likely to have been unconsciously inducted into the patriarchal and middle-class discourses and the Scottish Discursive Unconscious, despite their, in certain respects, diverse formation – Danischewsky was born in Russia, Rose and Mackendrick in the United States. However, the discourses, whether conscious or unconscious, set in play in the making of a film are not necessarily the same as those brought to bear on the reading of the completed film, as will be demonstrated in Chapter 3. Here the immediate concern is with the unconscious shaping of the film.

To be somewhat reductive, *patriarchy* is that ensemble of ideas, images, assumptions and prejudices within which it has come to seem natural that women are destined for less powerful roles in society than men. As Glenn Jordan and Chris Weedon put it:

> 'Natural' or 'normal' femininity and masculinity are defined in all areas of social life. Our identities as girls and boys, women and men, are formed in and through our involvement in social practices, from the family and schooling to culture, sport and the leisure industries. Cultural practices such as the media, marketing, the cinema, sport, art and popular culture construct forms of subjectivity which are mostly gendered ... Common sense tells us that women are intuitive, emotional, dependent, irrational, passive and weak. Men are rational, aggressive, independent and strong.[2]

As will be demonstrated, such ideas suffuse both the production processes and the textual fabrics of *Whisky Galore!* and *The Maggie*. It is so 'obvious' as scarcely to require comment that both films are structured primarily round conflicts between men (Macroon and Waggett in the former film, Marshall and Mactaggart in the latter), and that women largely occupy peripheral roles. But this very obviousness illustrates the extent to which male centrality has become *naturalized* as opposed to being *natural*. This was not at all unusual for films of this time (and, indeed, of our own time as well), but does not preclude the possibility of contradictions arising in the texts which may cast doubts on patriarchy or, at the very least, suggest – very likely unconsciously to the men making the films – that its maintenance is productive of a hysteria which manifests itself as artistic excess. Such a claim will be made with regard to *Whisky Galore!*

The rise of feminism over the last hundred years, and particularly over the last three decades, has meant that the diverse historical operation of particular patriarchies has been extensively documented. This is much less true of the historical construction of the class and ethnic discourses, even though within them the working class and the Scots, particularly the Highland Scots represented in these two films, are assigned roles analogous to those of women under patriarchy. Particularly with regard to class, however, the issue is rarely as simple as class representation. Although we can raise questions about, say, the class representation of Sergeant Odd in *Whisky Galore!* and the Wee Boy in *The Maggie*, the class discourse insinuates its way into these films in much more subtle ways: in the form of the music, perhaps, or the voice cadences and body language of particular actors. Important as the gender and class discourses are in relation to these films, however, it will be argued that the Scottish Discursive Unconscious is the dominant discourse, although all three discourses often intertwine as do the gender and ethnic discourses in the quotation from Compton Mackenzie which forms the rubric for this chapter. In what is far and away the most sophisticated account of the historical construction of the Scottish Discursive Unconscious, Malcolm Chapman notes:

> Since the eighteenth century, the Celtic fringes have posed for the urban intellectual as a location of the wild, the natural, the creative and the insecure. We can often find it said, with warm approval, that the Celts are impetuous, natural, spiritual, and naïve. I try in what follows to make it clear that such approval draws on the same system of structural

oppositions as is the accusation that the Celt is violent (impetuous, emotional), animal (natural), devoid of any sense of property (spiritual) or without manners (naïve) … We are dealing here with a rich verbal and metaphorical complex, and I have not thought it very important to distinguish between those who find a favourable opinion of the Gael within this complex, and those who dip into it to find the materials for derision. In both cases the coherence of the statements can only be found in their point of origin, the urban, intellectual, educated discourse of the English language and not at their point of application, the Celt, the Gael, the primitive who is ever departing, whether his exit be made to jeers or to tears.[3]

In short, the Celt (or, for our purposes, the Scot) is assigned a role in someone else's story designed to satisfy someone else's dreams, fantasies and fears. Analogously, this is true of women and the working class within the discourses which construct them. As Chapman and others (for example, Jeffrey Richards) have demonstrated, the Scottish Discursive Unconscious has been constructed over several centuries, its key architects including James 'Ossian' Macpherson, Sir Walter Scott, Felix Mendelssohn, Queen Victoria, Sir Edwin Landseer and Sir Harry Lauder. Within it a dream Scotland emerges which is highland, wild, 'feminine', close to nature and which has, above all, the capacity to enchant and transform the stranger, much as Sergeant Odd, the English soldier in *Whisky Galore!* and Calvin B. Marshall, the American tycoon in *The Maggie*, are transformed. Such a process is discernibly at work on the visiting Americans in *Brigadoon* and *Local Hero* as it was on (some at least of) the personnel making *Whisky Galore!* Danischewsky, describing his first encounter with Barra, true to the tradition of the Scottish Discursive Unconscious, observed that: 'in no time at all I had lost my heart to this enchanting island, and to the people who lived on it'.[4]

Progressively, the Scottish Discursive Unconscious has come to suffuse every sign system: literature, music, easel painting, photography, advertising, right down to film and television in our own day. As with the question of class and gender, its operation is never solely one of ethnic representation. At bottom there is the crucial question of the relationship between the representation and the socio-political reality of the place and people represented, although this should not be discussed in terms of 'truth to the real', but 'adequacy to the real'. It is a central contention of this book that *Whisky Galore!* (as both novel and film) and *The Maggie* were constructed – and largely read – within the Scottish Discursive Unconscious.

THE SHAPING OF *WHISKY GALORE!*

What is certain is that the film would not have existed without Mackenzie's original novel, the writing of which was the result of fundamental changes, largely self-wrought, in his own personal identity and politics. Born in West Hartlepool, the child of itinerant actors, he had by the outbreak of the Great War in 1914, settled into the persona not only of the English man of letters, but indeed of standard bearer of the great English literary tradition, being described by Henry James as 'the greatest talent of the new generation' which was coming to succeed Conrad, Galsworthy, Wells and Bennett, being admired by Scott Fitzgerald, Sinclair Lewis and Edmund Wilson and being told by the *Manchester Guardian* that 'the future of the English novel is to quite a considerable extent in his hands'. The choice of the term 'persona' is not accidental, it now being clear that Mackenzie's entire life consisted of a series of roles, two of which were to become particularly generative of *Whisky Galore!* In 1914 Mackenzie became a Roman Catholic and at the same time began laying the groundwork for the other key role in the novel's generation – that of Scotsman. Although his father's side of the family originated in Wester Ross, his family's London base, his public school education at St Paul's and his university education at Magdalen College, Oxford, made him a not untypical, if somewhat raffish, member of the English upper middle class. Nevertheless, his groping towards the identity of Scot is evident in his attempt to join the Seaforth High-landers in 1914 simply because they sported the Mackenzie tartan and it was around this time that he adopted the Mackenzie coat-of-arms and motto, *Luseo non Uro* ('I shine but I do not burn'), as ornament on the clasp of his cloak (another indication of his propensity for role-playing) and on his dinner service. He took to wearing the kilt when he lived in the Channel Islands in the early 1920s and visited Highland Scotland for the first time in 1926 when he was in his forties. As his biographer Andro Linklater writes:

> When at last he assumed the identity of a Scot, it was with the excitement of discovering what he felt to be his true self ... The emotion this Scotland aroused in him ran as deep as any he had felt since his adoles-cent conversion. In the mouth of John Ogilvie in *The North Wind of*

Love he described it as being as fundamental as that crucial experience. 'I love Scotland,' says Ogilvie, 'and whenever and wherever I feel that glow, it sets my heart beating as women in their day have set it beating. I had been stirred so profoundly by the abrupt revelation of life itself that the love I have for Scotland seems to me now the finest and perfect expression of my own vitality within the bounds of mortal flesh.'[5]

This Scottish identity which was romantic, Highland, Catholic and politically reactionary (Mackenzie had Jacobite sympathies and produced several ludicrous works advocating that cause) translated itself into a fourteen-year initial residence in Scotland, mostly on the Hebridean island of Barra (he was to return to Edinburgh in 1953 for the last two decades of his life); co-founding of the National Party of Scotland; and the production of extensive writings set in or related to Scotland, of which *Whisky Galore!* is one.

It is probable that Mackenzie's involvement with Scotland is one of the key factors in the virtually total eclipse of his reputation as a serious novelist. Compared with, say, D. H. Lawrence – with whom he was bracketed by Henry James and others – there has been virtually no critical interest in Mackenzie in recent years. The single excellent biography by Andro Linklater is joined by a mere handful of critical writings. This is partly due to the chameleon-like role-playing of Mackenzie himself. He was successively lay preacher, actor, serious man of letters, soldier, spy and later editor of *The Gramophone*, all-round journalist and radio and television personality. J. L. M. Stewart has described his

> almost preternatural vigour and fecundity. He might buy and sell islands like mad and pay for them by writing unending articles and reviews, interest himself in astrology, patronize cats … promote the sale of Scotch; associate pipes with tobacco as well as pibrochs, accept a commission from the Gas Board to write something called *The Vital Flame*, publish on his eightieth birthday the first of ten volumes of autobiography … To this day it is an open question where his true genius lay.[6]

Clearly, the main reason for Mackenzie's eclipse as a serious novelist was his spreading himself thin to sustain the extravagant lifestyle to which he had become accustomed, but this is not the whole story. Much of his 'Scottish' work – particularly the interlinked half-dozen books of which *Whisky Galore!* is one – were comic novels. Like his younger contemporary and fellow-Catholic, Graham Greene, who divided his works into serious novels and 'entertainments', Mackenzie was of a generation which maintained a rigid distinction between High and Popular Art – a distinction now regarded as infinitely less watertight – and saw his own Highland comedies as diversions from his more serious work. His autobiography records his putting aside, through ill-health, the writing of his 'serious' novel *The North Wind of Love* and dashing off the first of the Highland comedies, *The Monarch of the Glen* (1941). The others in the interlinked series are *Keep the Home Guard Turning* (1943), *Whisky Galore!* (1947), *Hunting the Fairies* (1949), *Ben Nevis Goes East* (1954) and *Rockets Galore!* (1957).

Despite Mackenzie's Hebridean domicile and his apparent engagement with Scottish culture, the issue of whether his Scots persona was genuine remains open. Linking him to other 'Scottish' novelists, Gavin Wallace states the problem succinctly:

> However separate in terms of background, creative personality and fictional priorities, [John] Buchan, Mackenzie and [Eric] Linklater are connected in that they remain prominent Scottish writers whose genuine affiliation to a national culture remains questionable, while their claims to be engaged with authentically Scottish preoccupations and themes can often appear dangerously spurious. In questioning the claims of these writers to the influence of what the novelist Muriel Spark has detected in her own work as 'a Scottish formation', commentators have alluded to the fact that the creative character of all three is marked by a tendency to indulge in an interplay between English and Scottish personae, a willingness to participate in the cultural, creative and political issues surrounding the [Scottish] Renaissance [of the 1920s] while indulging in the identifiably English mannerisms and overtones, in narrative style and lifestyle, against which so many Scottish writers of the time were reacting.[7]

Nothing symbolizes this tendency more than Mackenzie's impatient disengagement from the filming and marketing of *Whisky Galore!* in order to go off to the Indian sub-continent to research and write a history of the Indian Army. An ardent British imperialist all his life, he was an inveterate cultivator of aristocracy and royalty, particularly those with military connections. The problem is rendered more acute with Mackenzie because of his own clear-sightedness about some of the things that were wrong with Scottish culture. He was right on the mark when he described the Kailyard – that late nineteenth-century attempt at Scottish popular fiction, associated most notably with James Barrie – as having 'mortgaged Scottish literature to indignity' and he gives short shrift to that other regressive Scottish phenomenon, Tartanry, in *The North Wind of Love*. However, in outcome if not in intent, his Highland comedies, especially *Whisky Galore!*, have been encompassed within these same pernicious discourses:

> With the D.C. Thomson newspaper empire still producing its diet of post-Kailyard journalism, Munro-esque cartoon stereotypes in 'The Broons' and 'Oor Wullie' and pawky Scottishness in general, the novel *Whisky Galore!* shares the honours as one of Scotland's most conspicuous popular classics; a frequent subject of amateur theatricals, synonymous with the Hebrides, repeatedly cited as a reach-me-down metaphor for that most enduring of Scottish myths – whisky – a novel which answers perfectly those who would associate whisky and its mystical liturgy with some innate truth about the Scottish psyche. Most readers will be familiar with the images, on the covers of at least one of innumerable editions, of Lauderesque red-nosed and be-kilted Highland worthies genially soused from half-empty bottles of *Stag's Breath* dangling from sporrans, staggering in picturesquely Celtic fashion before a background of Hebridean sea and moonlight. Recent paperback editions of *Whisky Galore!* and its companions confirm that Mackenzie's image has without doubt found its niche within what might be generally described as the 'iconography' of popular Scottishness.[8]

Whether there is, indeed, as Wallace claims, an 'illustrative disparity between the film *Whisky Galore!* and the fictional text from which it derives' will loom large in the remainder of this chapter. Clearly there are enormous differences of content and style between novel and film. It is no secret that Mackenzie was displeased with the adaptation, displaying an almost fatalist resignation ('Another of my books gone west') about the cinema's capacity not only to adapt literature but to produce anything artistically serious, a position not untypical of an educated person of Mackenzie's generation. What seems to have irked him most was the film's ironing out of the novel's key religious opposition, shared with the other Highland comedies, that between Roman Catholicism and Protestantism, specifically that brand, Free Presbyterianism, so strongly rooted in the West Highlands and Islands. The religious divide between Great Todday and Little Todday, the imaginary islands of the novel, parallels the actual religious divide between the North and South Hebrides, Mackenzie himself being resident in Catholic Barra in the south. The excision of the religious rivalry (conflict would be too strong

1. *Mackenzie's novel marketed within 'the iconography of popular Scottishness'.*

a word for this most genial of stories) has the effect of removing several sub-plots (or, at least, important aspects of them) such as the decision of the English incomer Sergeant-Major Odd (Sergeant Odd in the film) to convert from Anglicanism to Roman Catholicism, and of removing one of the most engaging characters in the novel, Father Macalister, the Roman Catholic priest, with his passion for Wild West novels and flexible views about the morality of removing the whisky from the stricken ship. It has the effect also of removing the Presbyterian minister, Mr Morrison, whose anecdote communicates both the relaxed rivalry of Catholicism and Protestantism in the novel and the sly oneupmanship Mackenzie allows the former:

> 'Ah, well, I have a great respect for Father Macalister,' the Minister said. 'He's a great hand at teasing, though. I remember I once said to him … "We're all labourers in the same vineyard." And Father Macalister said – I thought it was rather witty, though it was against myself – "Ay," he said, "we're all labourers in the same vineyard, but it was we who planted the grapes."'[9]

Stylistically the novel is quite unlike the film, even allowing for the difference in medium. It is desultory and wholly lacking in narrative drive – the ship is not wrecked and the whisky removed until about halfway through the novel. It's central thrust is the creation of numerous 'couthy' characters. 'Couthy' is a Scots word with something of the same meaning as the English 'pawky'. It summons up a *mélange* of qualities among which a slightly tearful warm-heartedness is central. It is a word which sends Scots intellectuals into paroxysms of rage and has them, like Hermann Goering when confronted with the word 'culture', reaching for their Brownings. These 'couthy' characters exist in greater profusion in the novel than in the film, which telescopes several of them and drops many others. In the novel, much of the comedy turns on the linguistic specificity of the islanders, which Mackenzie recurrently attempts to render, as in the conversation Captain Mackechnie, master of the ferry plying among the islands, has with Sergeant-Major Odd when he learns he has travelled all the way up from Devonshire: 'You've had a long churney right enough, Sarchant. Teffonshire? That's a place I neffer was in. It's a crate place for cream, I believe.'[10]

It is an open question whether this, repeated *ad nauseam* throughout the novel, represents Mackenzie's rendering of the local manner of speaking or, as is common certainly in lowland Scotland, his having a laugh at the way the 'teuchtars' (as highlanders are disparagingly called) talk. The novel has an equally tedious recurrence in Odd's inability to pronounce *réiteach* (betrothal). On the other hand, as mentioned above, Mackenzie critiqued and satirized the regressive discourses of Tartanry and Kailyard and this critique is present in the novel in the form of the narrator's controlling discourse which was effectively untranslatable into the film. Across several of the Highland comedies, Mackenzie satirizes the writings of Alasdair Alpin Macgregor, whose books, to quote Gavin Wallace, are 'replete with ... Gaelic sentimentality and Celtic Twilight nebulosity'. Mackenzie invents a surrogate for Macgregor – Hector Hamish Mackay, author of *Faerie Lands Forlorn* and *Summer Days Among the Heather* – and quotes from him:

> 'Let us lean back in our deckchairs and watch the great sun go dipping down into the sea behind Little Todday ... And now behind us the full moon clears the craggy summit of Ben Sticla and swims south past Ben Pucka to shed a honey-coloured radiance over the calm water of the Coolish, as the strait between the two Toddays is called. Why, oh why, the lover of Eden's language asks, must the fair Gaelic word *Caolas* be debased by map-makers to Coolish, so much more suggestive of muni- cipal baths than of these "perilous seas". Alas, such sacrilege is all too sadly prevalent throughout Scotland. We turn our gaze once more to rest spellbound upon the beauty of earth and sea and sky and let our imagination carry us back out of the materialistic present into the haunted past.'[11]

As Wallace rightly observes, Mackenzie is here playing a dangerous game: 'This internalised rejection of popular Highland romanticism is a cunning ruse on Mackenzie's part for by mimicking the voice and values of another, he partly absolves himself from the responsibility of opening the gate to the Kailyard, as it were, and stepping through himself.'[12]

The key question is, of course, the extent to which both novel and film venture into the Kailyard and succumb to it or, to put it in the terms of the central theme of this book, the extent to which they are shaped within the Scottish Discursive Unconscious. As has been suggested, the parodic dimension of the novel may have been virtually untranslatable into the film although, as will be seen, the film may have had its own 'distancing' device drawn not from literature but from cinema itself.

There is one further dimension of *Whisky Galore!* as a novel (although it applies to the film as well) which requires discussion. It is part of what might be called its condition of intelligibility that it could only have been fashioned in a society within which not only is whisky extensively produced and consumed, but which has also evolved profound myths about whisky and its relation to bodily and mental health, to communal sociability and to the nature of manhood, all issues upon which whisky impinges in both novel and film. The posing of the idea that a whisky drought could be a cataclysmic event in a society structures the rhetoric of the opening chapter of the novel (and is reflected in the early part of the film). The novel begins with the return of Odd to the Islands but the chapter is structured round an enigma: what is it that those whom Odd encounters know that he does not? This is woven into several exchanges, as in one Odd has with the ferry captain:

> 'So long for the present, Captain. I daresay I'll be seeing you up at the hotel before we cross over to Kiltod.'
> 'I don't believe I'll be going up to the hotel this evening at all,' the skipper replied, his usually bright eyes clouded and curiously remote.[13]

What is clouding and rendering remote the skipper's eyes Mackenzie withholds from us. This is continued when Odd encounters Andrew Thomson, one of the characters dropped from the film. Thomson, a member of the Home Guard company to which Odd is to be attached as instructor, brings him up to date on its functioning:

> 'The turnout for shooting practice has been very poor all this month.'
> 'I expect they will be more keen as the spring comes along.'
> 'It's not the weather,' Andrew Thomson observed gloomily. 'There's another reason.' And then to prevent his companion's asking what that was he added hastily, 'I took Mrs Thomson over to Edinburgh on Friday.'[14]

Later, Thomson tells Odd:

> 'I'm afraid you'll find it kind of dull up at the hotel just now.'
> 'I won't find it dull. I'm looking forward to seeing a lot of old friends and having a jolly good Jock and Doris, as you call it, to celebrate getting back to the two tightest little islands in the world.'
> 'They're not very tight just now, Sergeant-Major,' he said, and went off quickly to find his bag.
> Sergeant-Major Odd puzzled for a moment over this remark.[15]

Later in the chapter the chilling fact, which up to that point none may speak, is revealed: there is no whisky on the Islands and none has arrived on the ferry. As well as signifying the mythic status of whisky in the novel (and film) and in the wider Scottish culture, the rhetorical device of non-revelation is entirely appropriate to the major ideological opposition in novel and film, the mutual incomprehension of Islanders and outsiders (particularly the English). Although in the novel and film this opposition is carried primarily in the Islanders versus Captain Waggett, with Odd as a kind of English defector to the Islanders' cause (symbolized in the novel by his conversion to Roman Catholicism and his marriage to an Island girl), since the novel begins with his return as an outsider, the mutual incomprehension motif can be activated immediately.

Enter Ealing Studios   Mackenzie was paid £500 down for the film rights of his novel, with a promise of a further £1,000 (which he did, indeed, receive) dependent on the film's profitability. He is also credited as co-writer, with Angus MacPhail, of the screenplay. The latter's name might suggest Scottish origins – Ivor Montagu described him as 'a red-haired and rather gauche Scot from Blackheath'[16] – but his English domicile and public-school and Cambridge education reveal him to have been formed within the English upper middle class. Certainly, the thumbnail sketch Charles Drazin offers of him in *The Finest Years: British Cinema of the 1940s* – with his solitary world bounded by the Ealing work that he despised, his passion for language games and rude seaside postcards, his aspiration to translate the classics of French literature and his drift (like his friend Robert Hamer) into alcoholism – rigorously excludes any concern with Scottish culture. On the other hand, one wishes to know more about the professional life of this seemingly pathetic figure who coined the term 'MacGuffin', invented the 'Memory Man' scene in *The 39 Steps* and was to go on to be credited as co-writer of two fine Hitchcock films of the 1950s, *The Man Who Knew Too Much* and *The Wrong Man*. The fullest account of the novel's acquisition by Ealing is contained in *White Russian, Red Face*, the autobiography of what would nowadays be called the film's line producer, Monja Danischewsky, who is credited as Associate Producer to Michael Balcon, Head of Production at Ealing. According to Danischewsky, Balcon reluctantly made him a producer to keep him at Ealing where he had served many years as Head of Publicity. That the opportunity presented itself in 1948 was due ultimately to the austerity of Britain at that time. Faced with an enormous balance of payments deficit, the British government, without consulting the film industry, added a 75 per cent customs tax to all imported films, most of which were, of course, American. The Motion

Picture Association of America responded by placing an embargo on all shipments of films to the UK. Faced with potentially blank screens and irate audiences, the government appealed to British film producers to increase production to fill the gap. Some years earlier, Balcon had entered into partnership with the more powerful Rank Organisation which now offered him additional finance with which to respond to the government's call. Wanting the cash, but not having the studio space or the in-house producers, Balcon concluded that the cash could be secured by promoting Danischewsky to producer and having him shoot the project of his choice (subject to Balcon's approval) on location. The idea of location shooting might perhaps be regarded as less original and bold than subsequently touted by the makers of the film. Cinephiles of the time were avidly consuming location-shot Italian neo-realist films such as *Rome, Open City* and *Paisà* which in turn influenced the emergence of American 'location thrillers' like *The Naked City*. Quite apart from the opportunity provided by the maladroit British government, location shooting was therefore 'in the air' in the late 1940s.

Danischewsky's book gives the impression that it was he who sought out Mackenzie's novel, but Charles Drazin, citing the minutes of the regular production meetings held at Ealing, reveals that, at the November 1947 meeting, it was Charles Frend who proposed the acquisition. Intriguingly, the minutes describe it as 'a modern Scottish story of the type for which we had been searching', suggesting that there were factors other than those outlined above which shaped *Whisky Galore!* An examination of production schedules of the time does indeed reveal that three other British films had been or were being (partially) shot on location in the Hebrides: *I Know Where I'm Going* (1945), *The Silver Darlings* (1947) and *The Brothers* (1947). So, it would appear that it was not only neo-realist-influenced location shooting that was 'in the air' at the time, but some kind of impulse towards things Scottish, possibly associated with the two hundredth anniversary of the Jacobite Uprising of 1745. That event was explicitly recalled in the ill-starred *Bonnie Prince Charlie* of 1948. Danischewsky records his surprise that film producers were not beating a path to Mackenzie's door to acquire the film rights to his book given its warm reception by the British press, but this may simply mean that the novel was already homologous with the Ealing values which Danischewsky, in common with other long-serving Ealing personnel, had doubtless internalized over the years. When the company left Ealing in 1955, Balcon had a plaque raised there which read 'Here, during a quarter of a century were produced many films projecting

Britain and the British character'. What he meant by this is summed up by that most sympathetic and perceptive of Ealing commentators, Charles Barr:

> Asked to invent a typical Ealing comedy plot, one might produce something like this. A big brewery tries to absorb a small competitor, a family firm which is celebrating its 150th anniversary. The offer is gallantly refused, whereupon the boss's son goes incognito from the big firm to infiltrate the small one and sabotage its fortunes. Gradually, he is charmed by the family brewery and by the daughter of the house, saves the company from ruin, and marries into it. Officials and workers unite at the wedding banquet to drink the couple's health in a specially created brew.
>
> To make this really Ealing, lay on the contrasts. The brewery names: Ironside against Greenleaf. Grim offices and black limousines against country lanes, ivy-covered cottages, horses, bicycles. Autocratic rule against the benevolent paternalism of a grey-haired old man who collects Toby Jugs. The beer itself: quantity against quality, machines against craftsmanship. The people and their manners: very harsh, very gentle. Small is beautiful.
>
> This, it will be guessed, is no invention. The film is called *Cheer, Boys, Cheer* and Balcon produced it at Ealing in 1939 ... a startling forerunner, a reminder that these later films [the famous Ealing comedies of the late 1940s and early 1950s] were not a sudden inspiration, but had roots and precedents.[17]

It scarcely needs to be pointed out how closely the ostensibly endorsed values of *Whisky Galore!* and *The Maggie* – it will be argued below that there are cracks and fissures between scripts and realization – conform to those in the above quotation. Two further brief quotations are necessary to round off Ealing (read Balconian) values. Talking to the critic John Ellis, Balcon described the Ealing community: 'By and large we were a group of liberal-minded, like-minded people ... we were middle-class people brought up with middle-class backgrounds and rather conventional educations.'[18] And Kenneth Tynan, in 1955, observed:

> Balcon has never made a film which paid any real attention to sex. His favourite productions – *The Captive Heart, Scott of the Antarctic, The Cruel Sea* – deal exclusively with men at work, men engrossed in a crisis, men who communicate with their women mainly by post card. A wry smile, a pat on the head, and off into the unknown: such is Ealing's approximation to sexual contact.[19]

While not *literally* true of *Whisky Galore!* and *The Maggie*, Tynan's remarks are certainly true in spirit. These then were the Balconian values internalized by the Ealing community and brought to bear in the shaping of individual projects, even though certain sensibilities – possibly Mackendrick's as opposed to T. E. B. Clarke's, for example – might feel more constrained, less naturally homologous with these values. Given that Mackenzie's class background and values were not dissimilar, *mutatis mutandis*, to Balcon's, the novel already fitted tolerably well into the Ealing mould, the reason, perhaps, why Danischewsky rather than other possible producers made a bid for it. (The minutes of the monthly Ealing production meeting of 9 June 1948 indicate that Danischewsky was already contemplating bidding for yet another of Mackenzie's Scottish comic novels, *Hunting the Fairies.*) There was one aspect of the novel which, it seems, Balcon was adamant should go, the religious division between Catholics and Protestants which is such an important part of *Whisky Galore!* and two of the other Highland comedies as well. Mackenzie was particularly irked by the ironing out of the religious differences in the novel to the extent of trying to have them reinstated at a late stage of the screenwriting process. The Islanders in the film are all sabbatarian Presbyterians and much humour is had from their being prohibited from going out to the wreck to retrieve the whisky until after the last stroke of midnight on the Sabbath. In the novel, the Presbyterians' anguish is heightened by the fact that their Catholic neighbours are under no such prohibition.

The shooting of the film involved an Ealing unit of eighty people on Barra for fourteen weeks, but bad weather meant that Danischewsky went £20,000 over budget (Balcon's wrath being assuaged only by the film's good box-office returns) and some of the 'exterior' scenes had to be shot in London at Ealing Studios. The extent to which Danischewsky's memoir is cast within the Scottish Discursive Unconscious is reflected in his numerous anecdotes about the pawkiness of the Islanders, and one passage reads like the account of a European anthropologist in some far-flung continent:

> We were all of us, I think, struck by the high level of intelligence of the Islanders. The art of conversation is kept alive in these remote places where conversation is one of the few entertainments to be indulged in after a day's work. That and reading. I was startled to be asked by a crofter whose home I was visiting, and who had come in covered with grime after a day's work on the road: 'I believe you're Russian?'

'Yes, I am.'

'I'm wondering if you can tell me why jealousy is such a recurring theme with Tolstoy's heroines?' I told him that *he* was probably in a better position to tell *me* why.[20]

Malcolm Chapman's observation that the otherness of the Celt may be signified by an apparently beneficent, but none the less controlling, discourse may be pertinent here. Also, underlying Danischewsky's anecdote, whether true or false, is the not untypical metropolitan yearning for the noble savage who is simultaneously in touch with both Nature and Culture. Philip Kemp records that the physical conditions of housing a unit of eighty had a good effect on the film, citing as an example that Joan Greenwood's living in the home of an Islander lent her accent a greater degree of authenticity. This may be true up to a point but, as will be argued below, the issue of her performance is more complicated than authenticity of accent.

Enter Alexander Mackendrick A reasonable picture of how, when and to what effect Mackendrick became involved in the pre-production shaping of the project can be gleaned from pulling together a number of accounts, most notably those of Danischewsky and Kemp. It seems that Mackendrick – who had joined Ealing in 1946 as a sketch artist after having worked mainly in advertising (he storyboarded several of the 1930s Horlicks 'night starvation' adverts, among others), cartoons and documentary films – was immensely keen to direct but that Balcon in particular was reluctant to assign him to a project being produced by a first-time producer. The minutes of the Ealing production meeting of 6 April 1948 record Balcon's advising Danischewsky to contact Pat Jackson, and the names of other directors, Basil Wright, Ralph Smart and Ken Annakin, are also mentioned. However, it seems that Danischewsky offered the director's chair to the more experienced Ronald Neame who turned it down, thereby making room for Mackendrick. Neame would have his chance later to activate the Scottish Discursive Unconscious in *Tunes of Glory* (his *The Prime of Miss Jean Brodie* is a more arguable case in which other discourses are at play). To indicate how unreliable screen credits often are (the script of *Whisky Galore!* is credited to Angus MacPhail and Compton Mackenzie) it seems that only the first draft was done by MacPhail and it was at this point that the Roman Catholic elements were excised. Danischewsky suggests that this was done not only for the Balconian reason of avoiding religious controversy, but to soup up the narrative as well, an understandable reason given the meandering quality of the novel. Since there is no mention of MacPhail having been part of the Ealing unit on Barra, it can be assumed that his involvement in scripting ended with the first draft. Philip Kemp takes up the story of the script's development:

> Together, Mackendrick and Danischewsky worked on further drafts of the script, tightening and refining the structure, before calling in Compton Mackenzie for final dialogue work. It was an approach to adaptation which Mackendrick found particularly fruitful. 'If you've got an original author, the thing is to take the subject entirely away from him and get it drastically rewritten by someone else – often the director if he's a writer-director. Then, when it's in fairly good shape, throw it back to the author for the final polish on dialogue. That way, you introduce a cinematic structure, which wasn't in the original, quite early on; but when the writer sees a new story brought back to him, he feels he can move in and make it his own, in colouring the speech and the language.' Mackenzie, after a few ritual grumbles ... undertook the final draft and for the price of a box of cigars threw in a few scenes lifted from *Keep the Home Guard Turning*.[21]

In fact, the scripting of the film may have been even more complex than this. For example, there are (in the Balcon papers held by the British Film Institute) contracts with three additional figures specifying various inputs to the film including contributions to the script. These are the writer Elwyn Ambrose; Donald Campbell, who had done a radio talk on the sinking of the 'S.S. Politician' (the event on which the novel is based); and the actor James Robertson Justice who appeared in the film. The latter's extant contract engages him not only on script work but on advising on local casting and locations as well. The scripting is further complicated by a reference in the minutes of the Ealing production meeting of 9 June 1948 to the effect that 'John Dighton was to give two weeks work to [the script of *Whisky Galore!*] before returning to *Kind Hearts and Coronets*'. The cumulative outcome of the adaptation and the diverse script revisions is the dropping of several characters, the compositing of others, the refocusing on action as much as character –– Waggett's opposition to the Islanders' stealing of the whisky is worked up into a narratively swift retrieval, hiding and search for the whisky – and the foregrounding of only two relationships, that between Sergeant Odd and Peggy and that between George Campbell and his mother. The central narrative device of the search for the hidden whisky involves, of course, the novel and film's key ideological opposition – that between Waggett and the Islanders.

Both Danischewsky and Kemp record the considerable tension which existed between Danischewsky and Mackendrick:

> Filming was also bedevilled by disagreements between producer and director – hardly unusual, except that in this case the point at issue was the film's moral stance. While working on the script, Danischewsky 'discovered to my horror that [Mackendrick] really disapproved of the Islanders taking the whisky. No real moral sanction could be found for it.' Consequently, 'as our work on the film progressed, Sandy found himself more and more in sympathy with Captain Waggett'. Mackendrick puts it rather differently. 'I began suddenly to realise that the most Scottish character in *Whisky Galore!* is Waggett the Englishman. He, if you like, is the only Calvinist, puritan figure, who's against looting and so on – and all the other characters aren't Scots at all, they're Irish.' He accordingly suggested that Waggett, alone of the cast, should wear a kilt, 'which is of course ersatz Scots, an invention of Prince Albert'. Danischewsky turned the idea down, feeling its subtlety would be lost on all but Scottish audiences.[22]

Danischewsky, elsewhere in his memoirs, implies that Mackendrick *was* Calvinist, citing his 'strictly Calvinist upbringing by a stern grandmother in Glasgow' (to which Mackendrick had gone to live from the United States at the age of sixteen). Whether or not this is true, the above quotation raises several interesting points. Mackendrick's attack on ersatz Scottishness parallels Mackenzie's similar attacks, in the novel and elsewhere, with the possibility that Mackendrick might similarly have become trapped – through the workings of the Scottish Discursive Unconscious – in a terrain where the only meaning possible was an ersatz Scottish meaning, the way Mackenzie's Scottish comic novels are now marketed and read. Second, assuming that the prime motive, at the scripting stage, for the excision of the Roman Catholic elements – leaving all the Islanders as sabbatarian Presbyterians – was narrative clarity, the excision removed any possibility of constructing them as 'Irish' (though there may lurk here in Mackendrick's words a somewhat questionable stereotype of Irish identity). Finally, it is an open question, which only detailed attention to the film's *mise-en-scène* might have a hope of resolving, whether Mackendrick's alleged sympathy for Waggett is embodied in the film as we have it.

To complicate the question of the meaning of the film and to whom responsibility for that meaning should be attributed, Balcon was so dissatisfied with the completed film that he was prepared to cut it to one hour and release it as a second feature. It seems that another more experienced Ealing director, Charles Crichton, shot some additional footage, took it and the film as shot into the cutting room and (Crichton claims in consultation with Mackendrick) emerged with the film as we now have it.

The complicated history of *Whisky Galore!*'s production should, at the very least, make us wary of celebrating it, in auteurist terms, as an unambiguously Mackendrick film.

THE SHAPING OF *THE MAGGIE*

If one were attempting to relate *The Maggie* to the moment when it was produced, one would be obliged to talk about the escalating intrusion of American capital(ism) into post-war Europe, not least Scotland. David Forsyth, who has studied the phenomenon as it relates particularly to Scotland, has revealed that in 1939 there were only five US-owned firms in Scotland whereas by 1954 there were twenty-eight. He also notes that they were much more *visible* than the older, British-owned firms:

> Most of the US firms are of recent vintage and operate in new, impressive factories far removed in both appearance and situation from the bulk of Scottish industry. The greater emphasis placed by US-owned firms on public relations activities and on being – and being seen to be – 'good citizens' has reinforced the tendency for firms that are new, large and different to attract more attention than indigenous operations.[23]

What this meant in concrete terms is that the Scottish press (the national but more particularly the local) in the early 1950s was full of stories about larger-than-life American executives – not at all unlike Calvin B. Marshall – making a splash in their local communities. Appropriately, Pusey – the stereotypical middle-class Englishman – is Marshall's public relations officer and the tycoon's concern for PR is evident in his conversations with Fraser, the Glasgow newspaperman who avidly reports every stage of Marshall's humiliation. Philip Kemp has quite rightly linked the name of the American both to Marshall Aid – the post-war financial mechanism named after the American soldier and statesman George C. Marshall and designed to bind (Western) Europe into the American sphere of influence – and to the 'Protestant Ethic', said to underpin capitalism in general and American capitalism in particular

2. *A clash of cultures: American tycoon; Scottish puffer.*

and to be particularly active within the Calvinist strain of Protestantism. It will be necessary to keep this dimension in mind when we come to discuss an important American response to *The Maggie* and in relation to the Scottish Discursive Unconscious, it being recalled that the latter relates only partly to the way Scots are represented but perhaps more importantly to the gulf between that representation and the historical reality of Scotland.

There is a perhaps unconscious element which may have shaped *The*

Maggie. Living in Scotland from the age of sixteen, Mackendrick is quite likely to have been exposed to the *Para Handy* tales of Neil Gunn, stories which, like *The Maggie*, revolve round the crew of a Clyde puffer. Jeffrey Richards – making the argument that the central point about popular literature and film is, precisely, that they are *popular* – quotes John Grierson's response to a 1959 television adaptation of the *Para Handy* tales (there have been two subsequent adaptations, the last starring Gregor Fisher of *Rab C. Nesbitt* fame):

> an Odyssey of the common man with all his prides and all his humours … Where its appeal lies … is that it is the epic of the non-metropolitan. It's a tale that crops up a lot in the Scottish mind, and, of course, in Scottish writing. You get it with Linklater in *Laxdale Hall*. You get it with Compton Mackenzie in *Whisky Galore!*[24]

This is a description which would certainly accommodate the story outline of *The Maggie*, although neither the *Para Handy* stories nor their television adaptations reached the pitch of delirium and bleakness of certain aspects of the film.

The production history of *The Maggie* is paradoxical. On the one hand, it is altogether less well documented than that of *Whisky Galore!* but, on the other hand, Mackendrick's control of the project right from the start is less equivocal. It is the only picture on which he received screen credit for writing the original story. Although there is no massively present and commented-upon novel as the original source, as in the case of *Whisky Galore!*, there is a vestigial connection with Compton Mackenzie since it seems that Mackendrick got the idea for the story from hearing Mackenzie's account (he was a marvellous raconteur) of his difficulty in transporting his library to Barra. Mackendrick was apparently greatly taken with

> the near criminal irresponsibility of the captain and crew of the vessel involved. And I was struck by the character conflict between Mackenzie, an internationally famous figure, and this crew of rascally freebooters … It was this that led me to explore the 'puffers'. These ocean-going tramp steamers, I discovered, are regarded by the islanders and the Glasgow shipping industry with a mixture of hilarious contempt and some affection … Quite early in developing a structure for the story, I made the decision to replace Compton Mackenzie with an American character and to establish him as an efficiency-minded executive in an airline company. There were two clear advantages: an American star is

attractive to British film distributors; second it obviously sharpened the dramatic conflict.[25]

It seems Mackendrick got help with the third act from a childhood friend who recalled an actual story about a puffer which ran aground and was saved by jettisoning its cargo. It was at this point that William Rose, at his request (he had read Mackendrick's story), came aboard as screenwriter; the screenwriting credit is solely his, Mackendrick not being mentioned in this category – not unusual in the film industry, even when the director (and, indeed, the producer) may have been heavily involved in writing the script. Also, in comparison with the well-documented background to the making of *Whisky Galore!*, we have no Danischewsky-style memoir from *The Maggie*'s producer, Michael Truman. Possibly the most anonymous figure in the entire Ealing line-up, Truman is known to have entered the film industry in 1934, to have produced army training films during the war and to have joined Ealing as an editor in 1944. He went on to become a producer in 1951 and a director in 1955, but his films in both roles have never attracted any kind of critical interest, nor does he figure in other people's accounts (as does, for example, Danischewsky in Mackenzie's memoirs) as a source of tension or strong opinions. That certainly could not be said of William Rose who is spoken of in several interviews (including some with Mackendrick) as hot-tempered and difficult to work with. If Mackendrick is the Scot born in America, Rose is the American who came to live in Britain, for some years in Scotland itself. It has been said of him that he was an Ealingite even before he came to work for Ealing, the film *Genevieve*, about a vintage British car, being offered as evidence, though it is usually added that he should be bracketed with Mackendrick as being on the dark side of Ealing, that side which found some nasty toads in the cosy Ealing garden. As Philip Kemp puts it, 'there can be sensed in Rose's scripts an edge of exasperation at the obstinate British attachment to discomfort and inefficiency for their own sake'. In addition to *The Maggie*, Rose was to write four films for Ealing, *Touch and Go*, *The Ladykillers*, *Man in the Sky* and *Davy* (*The Ladykillers* also being directed by Mackendrick). Philip Kemp cites an interview with Mackendrick in which he gives some indication of Rose's input to the scripting of *The Maggie*:

> one of the things he'd done was almost eliminate one of the sub-plots. In my draft the wife [of Marshall] appears about half way through: there's a cutaway during a phone call and it's clear she's thinking of

leaving him. And then she turns up again at the end. Now he's been trying to bribe her to stay with him; but it's just because he's thrown away the bribe, by sacrificing the cargo, that she decides to stay. So in the end she rewards him for all the humiliation he's suffered – and that's the key thing that could have made the film a popular success. Bill cut that out – but I didn't really notice because the script was so well-written.[26]

It is suggested – in the next chapter's analysis of *Whisky Galore!* – that the demented laughter (from Waggett's wife) on which the film closes might have been a (possibly unconscious) borrowing from the ending of *The Treasure of the Sierra Madre* which was much discussed at the time of *Whisky Galore!*'s making. This possibility is recognized in the axiom that films are made as much from other films as from 'life'. It is just possible that, at a more general level (although this is not documented anywhere), another film 'shadowed' the making of *The Maggie*. That film is *The African Queen*, the events of which take place largely on a boat not dissimilar to the puffer in *The Maggie*. *The African Queen* was very much 'in the air' at the time *The Maggie* was being formulated and put into production, having been a resounding commercial and critical success and netting an Oscar for its star, Humphrey Bogart. Again, being speculative, perhaps a successful film about a small boat being 'in the air' and the success, five years previously, of Ealing's only other Scottish project, *Whisky Galore!*, favourably disposed Michael Balcon towards the making of *The Maggie*. What is on record, however, in the minutes of the meetings held each month by Ealing's producers and directors, is their awareness of what other production set-ups were doing. During a discussion of the possibility of making *Three Men in a Boat* at the meeting of 8 July 1948, 'it was suggested that if the subject were to be made it should be on the lines of *Meet Me in St Louis*'.

There is a marked paucity of background evidence about the origins and the making of *The Maggie*. To illustrate one dimension of the research problem, the above discussion of *Whisky Galore!* makes frequent reference to the minutes of the monthly production meetings held by senior Ealing personnel. The obvious place to look for this material is in the extensive collection of Michael Balcon's papers held by the British Film Institute. However, these crucial documents are missing from the Balcon papers and are only partially replaced by a brief run of the minutes, covering the period of *Whisky Galore!*'s production, in the Ivor Montagu papers (also held by the BFI). The minutes for the period

covering *The Maggie*'s gestation and production are missing from the
Montagu papers as well. What little evidence there is tells us less about
the film itself than about the development of 'showbiz' journalism in
the four years separating *Whisky Galore!* and *The Maggie*. This is true
about what we would nowadays call the tabloid press – but, since this
was a later term indicating page size, is better called the popular press
– and the local press. The increase of gossipy showbiz columns in these
sectors of the press in the 1950s led to the increased servicing of such
columns by all the studios in the form of more numerous and regular
press releases trailing their upcoming films, usually in the form of
'human interest' stories and anecdotes about the personnel involved,
most often the actors and particularly the stars. There is a significant
increase of extant material of this kind on *The Maggie* and much of it
is symptomatic of the kind of 'knee-jerk' way such columns operated,
very often reproducing verbatim the stories circulated in the studio press
releases with some crude chopping – it could not be dignified with the
term 'editing' – to meet local exigencies of space. The cuttings file on
The Maggie in the British Film Institute contains material from as far
afield as Edinburgh and Bristol all containing the same anecdote about
how wet Paul Douglas got shooting a brief outdoor scene in Glasgow
and how Hubert Gregg had to borrow a raincoat from a local reporter
and had to hang on to it for subsequent scenes to observe continuity.
Such columns, especially in the national popular papers, often highlight
the paper's own columnist as much as the personnel from the film
ostensibly being reported on, insinuating that they have a special access
to the stars. Such is the case with David Lewin's 'Spotlight' column in
the *Daily Express*. One such column is entitled 'Mr Douglas has puffer
trouble on the loch' and exemplifies a phenomenon which was to become
increasingly common in this kind of journalism: the location report.
This piece – illustrated by a photograph of Douglas and Lewin on the
set – is mainly about the bad weather on Islay during shooting, but
deals anecdotally with Douglas and Tommy Kearins, the fourteen-year-
old Glasgow schoolboy who plays Douggie, the Wee Boy in the film.
Given that such material rarely produces significant information about
the film it is ostensibly dealing with, the critic/historian is left with the
shooting script and the film itself.

TWO
Inside *Whisky Galore!* and *The Maggie*

'I can't bear professional Scotsmen.' (Alastair Sim on turning down the role of Joseph Macroon in *Whisky Galore!*)

'I think it's a very phoney, un-Scottish film; it's a parody of Scots people.' (Alexander Mackendrick on *Whisky Galore!*)[1]

In 1982, in an essay about the screen representation of Scotland and the Scots, the present writer dealt with the numerous films which had been the staple production of Films of Scotland, the body set up to encourage filmmaking in Scotland and which was deeply marked by the Griersonian documentary tradition emanating from its founding director, Grierson's friend and biographer, Forsyth Hardy. The essay went on:

> From among these films it would be possible to construct, Frankenstein-monster like, the Ur-Tartan Documentary. It would open, accompanied by a clarsach or plaintive Scottish violin tune, on a panorama of lochs and bens, preferably in autumn since the lament is the dominant tone of the form. Against this Landseerian background ... the commentary begins to unfold. The choice of narrator is crucial: the voice must call up the cluster of motifs characteristic of the genre: beauty, sadness, dignity, loss.[2]

In 1990, speaking about *Whisky Galore!* at a French film festival, Mackendrick told the audience, 'I hope you realize it's a parody of a documentary.' In the last chapter it was pointed out that certain aspects of the novel's framing narration – most notably the arch-romantic discourse of Mackenzie's invented travel writer, Hector Hamish Mackay – raised the possibility that this was the author's way of distancing himself from the very terrain he had to enter – populist humanism expressed in a range of lovable, 'couthy' Scots characters – in order to write a popular comic novel about the Highlands. It was also suggested that this device was effectively untranslatable into the film without doing violence to the popular, classical narrative aesthetic it operates within, but that the film might have its own way, by recourse to the history of cinema, of signifying some distance from the popular narrative it was itself embarking upon. Bearing in mind Mackendrick's words at the French film festival, it is tempting to see the opening of the film precisely in these terms. At the level solely of the image, the film would seem to be conforming to the kind of documentary described above, though in black and white since colour had not yet become standard by 1949. The background to the credits is a series of sea- and shore-scapes accompanied by the kind of bouncy music which tells us we are in the presence of a comedy. Ernest Irving's musical score is based on diverse Scottish folk songs in which the 'Scotch Snap' musical form (the international musical form for signifying Scotland) is prominent, and played by the Philharmonia Orchestra. The use of a classical orchestra is entirely typical of the 1940s and itself produces a kind of (unconscious) alienating effect, rather like hearing Dame Kiri Te Kanawa singing songs from *West Side Story*; that is, there is a lack of fit between the musical technique and the material or, in the case of the film's score, between the musical technique and the milieu. This is part of a wider problem needing deeper investigation, the dominance in British cinema up to and including the 1940s of middle-class ways of seeing and hearing the world, a phenomenon also discernible in actorial performance. Music and performance are two of the ways in which an unconscious class discourse may have found its way into films. Inexplicably, as the names of Michael Balcon, Alexander Mackendrick, the Ealing logo and the rubric explaining that the events depicted are based on a real incident, appear on the screen, the score elides into a kind of bland salon music. It is at this point that the parody of traditional documentaries about Scotland (indeed, about any 'primitive' society) begins. The first few images of crashing seas, accompanied by 'dramatic' music, are very reminiscent of Robert Flaherty's *Man of Aran*, but it is with the introduction of the commentary that the flavour of the Ur-Tartan Documentary emerges. It is delivered by Finlay Currie, a Scottish actor whose physically imposing presence and resonant, somewhat sanctimonious voice led to his being cast as an aged patriarch in films set in the Scottish past and in biblical epics. His mellifluous voice tells us that

North-west of Scotland, on the broad expanse of the Atlantic, lie the lovely islands of the Outer Hebrides; small, scattered patches of sand and rock rising out of the ocean. To the west there is nothing except America. The inhabitants scrape a frugal living from the sea, the sand and the low-lying hills of coarse grass and peat bog, a happy people with few and simple pleasures.

This parodically banal commentary is accompanied by stereotypical images of, for example, a fisherman mending his nets and his smiling wife at a spinning wheel before a thatched cottage. There is even the characteristically inane music that usually accompanies such images. At one level the sequence is actually giving concrete information to an audience which does not know where the Hebrides are. The parodic element comes in the disjuncture between Currie's plangent words and some of the images accompanying them. For instance, against the words 'the inhabitants scrape a frugal living from the sea' there is an image of a well-fed fisherman holding up a meaty lobster, and counterpointing the words 'a happy people with few and simple pleasures' nine children of diverse ages run from the thatched cottage.

As the discussion in the last chapter indicated, it is often difficult to assign responsibility to particular personnel for what appears in the finished film and to ascertain at what stage 'creative' decisions were taken. This is particularly acute with regard to *Whisky Galore!* from what we know of the extensive reshaping, involving Charles Crichton, some time after the unit returned from Barra. Fortunately, however, the British Film Institute holds a shooting script dated 16 July 1948, which must have been written very close to (if not indeed within) the time of shooting. It is headed 'REVISED SHOOTING SCRIPT' (hereafter RSS) and a note indicates that it is 'subject to alteration in the FINAL SHOOTING SCRIPT'. As far as is known, no copies of the latter survive. The RSS contains the parodic sequence as we have it in the film but, interestingly, it does not constitute the opening of the film in the RSS. There is a discarded sequence which reads:

TITLES
The background to the lettering is a series of dissolving aerial shots taken from an aircraft flying north and represent a journey from London to the Hebrides.

First the plane flies low over the crowded city –
then over green fields –
over low-lying hills –

over the peaks of the lake district –
over the Western highlands.

The aircraft is now flying at a considerable height over the Atlantic. At
the top of the screen appears an island. Losing height, we begin to
descend to it. Music over the scene has been loud, stirring and Scottish
in character.

It is at this point that the parody documentary scene begins in the
RSS with the words: 'Commentary (A deep voice with no more than a
trace of Highland intonation).' Clearly, this sequence was conceived to
orient the audience geographically to the locale, but that function is
performed by the commentary, rendering the above sequence redundant.
Also, it may have been deemed confusing since sequences of planes
arriving usually involve the disembarkation of some figure central to
the narrative (as in, for example, the opening sequence of *Triumph of
the Will*) which is not the case in *Whisky Galore!* However, the dropping
of this aerial sequence has an effect that the filmmakers were almost
certainly unaware of: it further represses the already deeply sedimented
Scottish Discursive Unconscious. By structuring the sequence as 'a
journey from London to the Hebrides' the film was implicitly stating
that the point of utterance of the story, the controlling vision, was that
of London, of Ealing Studios, rather than its point of application, the
land and people of Hebridean Scotland. As we have put it previously,
the (Highland) Scots are once more figures in someone else's story.

Towards its close, the commentary in the film as we have it begins to
encompass the central theme by telling us that though the Islanders live
far from cinemas and dance halls, they know how to enjoy themselves
and they have everything they need. This is accompanied by an image
of communal whisky drinking in a bar. Suddenly, however, the mood
changes, the sun-drenched seas and shores give way to dark and angry
skies, with suitably dramatic music accompanying them. The cadences
of Currie's commentary change as well: 'But in 1943 disaster over-
whelmed this little island. Not famine, nor pestilence, nor Hitler's bombs,
nor the hordes of an invading army', counterpointed with a discarded
spinning wheel beside the thatched cottage and the wan face of a child
looking from a window, ' ... but something, far, far worse'. The last
three words are punctuated by increasingly intense and discordant
snatches of music, then the owner of the bar, the light glinting on his
spectacles, announces: 'There is *no* whisky!'

Against intense music, a poleaxed Islander, in close-up, receives the news and stumbles from the bar as Currie, on the commentary, states the central myth of the film: 'Whisky. *Uisge beatha*. The water of life. And to a true Islander, life without whisky is just not worth living.'

Many of the changes from the RSS to the film as we have it seem designed to make the narrative proceed apace. Such is the case with Captain Macphee, the poleaxed Islander who literally cannot live without whisky. The process of his dying is much more extended in the RSS than in the film and, in particular, one unusually imaginative scene inserted very late in the writing process (it is recorded as 'new page 6' and on different coloured paper) has been jettisoned. Macphee, stumbling back to his house to die, is confronted by the following vision: 'Silhouetted against the dark skyline is a White Horse. For a fleeting moment it dissolves into the trademark on a whisky label but before the image is clearly visible it fades again to the real horse which tosses its head and whinnies again. Macphee averts his eyes quickly from this harrowing sight, continues on his way.'

In the film, Macphee's leaving the bar is followed by his expiring in his bed. The camera, accompanied by harp music, pans and tilts upwards and there is a dissolve to a celestial sky, followed by the pulling down of a blind. Currie's voice once more comes in with a nicely ambiguous metaphor – 'From that day every man went into mourning. Mourning for a departed spirit' – as another dissolve takes us into the dead man's wake which is lit like a German Expressionist film and introduces us to the characteristically *populated* frame of *Whisky Galore!*, an early indication of a control over screen space, the placing of actors and the choreographing of movement which Mackendrick was to develop and deploy to such devastating effect in *The Maggie*. The wake scene ends with the frame moving to reveal George Campbell (Gordon Jackson) and his morose verbal exchange with Joseph Macroon which sets in train one of the two major sub-plots of the film, George's intended marriage to Joseph's daughter Catriona and the trouble this will cause with George's mother. Interestingly, although the film is constructed formally within the movement to two marriages (more accurately betrothals since, unlike in the novel, we do not see the marriages take place), the emphasis is not on the relationship between George and Catriona, but between George and his mother. The narrative economy of the film is such that in barely five minutes it has outlined the setting, stated the mythical premise of the narrative about the centrality of whisky, and set up one of the major sub-plots. However, the way it does this poses interesting contrasts between novel and film, suggesting that they might have been preoccupied with different questions. Where the novel requires the lengthy rhetorical literary device of creating an enigma for Sergeant Odd to convey the mythic status of whisky, the film accomplishes this by the much more economical cinematic means of having a character expire for want of it; that is, the film shows rather than tells. Also, the film reverses the weighting the novel gives to the two marriage sub-plots. Instead of introducing Odd first, it introduces George, suggesting that the film is interested in his relationship with his mother more than the somewhat bland Odd/Peggy relationship. This is to some extent reflected in the casting, Gordon Jackson being, even at this early stage of his career, a more prominent player than the actor who plays Odd, Bruce Seton. The casting of Joan Greenwood as Peggy also suggests that, at some stage of the project, the Odd/Peggy relationship was regarded as more important. It is intriguing to speculate whether this apparent 'deformation' of the film's intentions in favour of the George/Mrs Campbell relationship might relate to Mackendrick's alleged Calvinism, the animating feature of that relationship. Mackendrick's shift of attention from the ostensible star, Joan Greenwood, is to some extent compensated for by a narratively pointless emphasis on her in the *réiteach* sequence which ends the film.

The arrival of the ferry, which incident opens the novel, follows almost immediately from the wake with a brief scene introducing Peggy and Catriona (Gabrielle Blount) and marks the setting-up of the second major sub-plot, the Odd/Peggy relationship. The arrival of the ferry in the film, although it contains vestiges of the impulses in the novel, is reworked to introduce the central figure of the film, Captain Waggett (Basil Radford), and to set in train the basis of the film's major plot: Waggett's arrogance, his outsider's view and his incomprehension of the Islanders' way of life as expressed in his seeking to recover the purloined whisky. He is introduced only very briefly in the second chapter of the novel: 'Paul Waggett was the retired stockbroker who had bought Snorvig House and rented the shooting of the two islands from the Department of Agriculture. He commanded the Home Guard Company and in the opinion of the Islanders never allowed himself to run out of creature comforts.'[3]

Curiously, Waggett is not described in the RSS, although his wife Dolly is: 'a worried little woman who seems to carry all her husband's burdens as well as her own and is distresed when he takes further responsibilities'.

In the film, Waggett is seen in his domestic setting and in his relation-

3. *George Campbell (Gordon Jackson) confronted by his mother (Jean Cadell). The bagpiping patriarch is on the wall behind her.*

ship with Dolly, his condescending attitude being faithfully transposed from novel to film:

'Mr Morrison really ought to keep that cold of his to himself.'

'I know, dear, I think it's so selfish the way people scatter colds all over the place. I do hope you've caught it in time.'

'You mean "not caught it," Dolly,' said her husband with that superior smile which sent his sharp nose up in the air.[4]

Again, with great narrative economy, the film brings Waggett from the domestic setting to the pier for an altercation with the captain of the ferry which reveals him as a pettifogging book soldier. The casting of Basil Radford in the role of Waggett is inspired. Previously he and Naunton Wayne had appeared in several films – most notably Hitchcock's *The Lady Vanishes* – as a pair of archetypal middle-class Englishmen who believe England to be the centre of the world and cannot understand why, for example, foreign newspapers do not report Test Match scores. His Waggett is a harder-edged version of this same persona. It will be recalled that, in Danischewsky's view, as the filming progressed, Mackendrick became more sympathetic to Waggett, but this view is difficult to sustain in light of what is actually on the screen, particularly the ending, of which more presently.

Having set up the central characters and relationships, the film then shows where its major interest really lies by opting once more for the relationship between George Campbell and his mother – another piece of inspired casting in Jean Cadell – appropriately referred to and addressed throughout the film as 'Mistress Campbell'. As described in the novel, Mrs Campbell is 'a large, majestic old woman, with icy pale blue eyes and a deep husky voice'[5] but in the film, incarnated in Jean Cadell, she is a shrieking termagant. Although George is in his mid-thirties, he lives in mortal terror of his mother and jumps to her every command. Having learned about George's proposal to Catriona, she hauls him out of the class he is teaching and confronts him. In response to his evasive comment that he meant to tell her but heard the news himself only yesterday, she deploys the chilling lines taken almost verbatim from the novel:

> 'Do you mean to stand there, George, and tell me you'd not been thinking about that girl until yesterday afternoon?'
> 'I'd thought about her, yes … '
> 'Then why was I kept in the dark about your thoughts?'

The excision from the film of the Catholic versus Protestant motif of the novel poses certain problems for the film. Mackenzie's detestation of Protestantism, particularly the Free Presbyterian variety, was so intense that it drove him to create one of the most darkly forceful characters in the novel, Mrs Campbell, whose sanctimonious, hell-ridden tirades could be set against the genial casuistry of the Catholics. In the film all the Islanders are of one faith, Free Presbyterianism. Mrs Campbell, the girls Peggy and Catriona and the men who steal the whisky from the wreck are all supposedly adherents of an unbending theology, which produces incongruities in their behaviour. As Free Presbyterians the girls would not have been permitted, as their father Joseph puts it, 'stick lips and cigarettes', nor would Joseph and the other men have been allowed to purloin the whisky; indeed, it is doubtful if it would have passed their lips although, needless to say, Calvinism is an excellent breeding ground for hypocrisy. The strong tendency of Calvinism is to split communities into the elect and the damned. Mackendrick's Islanders are made to behave like the Catholic Islanders in the novel, which contrasts with their rigidity on the issue of Sunday observance when they cannot approach

4. *Alexander Mackendrick rehearses the 'chaste' love scene with Joan Greenwood and Bruce Seton.*

the wreck until the last stroke of midnight on the Sabbath. In the film dramatic necessity triumphs over behavioural and doctrinal consistency.

There are several quasi-love scenes in the novel, with Odd thinking wistfully about Peggy and, on occasion, embracing her. In true Ealing style, however, the only love scene in the film is, on the whole, a chaste affair. Odd and Peggy walk on the beach and he asks her to marry him. The twenty-year gap in their ages in the novel is reduced to sixteen years in the film, although even this may have added to the built-in Ealing reticence about sex. Cinema has always had difficulty in seeing inter-generational sex as anything other than predatory. On the beach Joan Greenwood deploys the teasing sensuality that is her hallmark and tells Odd that she could not possibly consider marrying him until he asks her in Gaelic, which he then does – another step on the way to his identifi-cation with the Islanders. Much of the scene is played in two-shot and close-ups of both actors, with Peggy laid back quite sensually on the sand, but when she accepts his proposal, instead of the subsequent kiss being shown in two-shot, Odd bends down out of frame and the kiss, if there is one, occurs off-camera. The RSS reveals that this exclusion of on-screen sexuality had been planned right from the start. It reads: 'ODD looks down at her for a moment then he leans down to kiss her. CAMERA DOES NOT MOVE, so that as his head goes out of frame, the focus changes and we are left on a vista of the Hebridean coastline.'

5. *A calculating look in her eye. Joan Greenwood as Peggy Macroon.*

The next shot is, however, rather more ambiguous about sexuality: 'Another vista of the coastline ... In the distance we see two small figures climbing to the top of the sand dunes. They are so far away as to be hardly recognisable. But the girl is seen to stoop putting on her shoes. Then they join hands and start to walk inland.'

It is intriguing to speculate that, socialized into the known Ealing (or Balconian) attitude to sexuality on screen, the writer(s) of the script, including Mackendrick, are here signifying sexuality rather obliquely. This view achieves even more credence since, in the film as we have it, a shot of horses on the seashore has been interposed between the above two shots from the RSS.

Apart from giving an indication of how sexuality is handled in (most) Ealing films, the scene raises questions about Joan Greenwood's playing of Peggy. Danischewsky saw it as a triumph of authenticity due to Greenwood's good ear for accents since, like other members of the unit, she lived with a local family during shooting. There is some truth in this solely at the linguistic level, but it is hard to differentiate her eye and body movements as Peggy from those she deployed as, say, Sibella in *Kind Hearts and Coronets*. That is, what we see coming into play in this scene is the (unconscious) process of middle-class theatrical training and practice; like the question of the musical score, the assertion of the unconscious middle-class discourse in *Whisky Galore!* A later scene, in which she opens the door for a raiding exciseman, is an even better example of Greenwood's 'jarring' performance as is her bearing in the dance sequence at the *réiteach* in which the calculating look which is never far from her eyes is most evident.

Up to this point in the film, we have seen Waggett only twice, both in scenes the dramatic purpose of which is to underscore his impatience with the Islanders and his utter incomprehension as to what makes them tick. We have referred to his argument with the ferry captain. The second time he appears he is supervising the operation of a roadblock designed to halt enemy movement on the island's only road. Sergeant Odd points out, to Waggett's chagrin, that since there is only one road, would not the enemy simply turn round and approach from the opposite direction. Seeing Odd as a fellow-Englishman – albeit of a lower social class (Odd's constant 'yessiring', in form rather than substance, represents another intrusion of the class discourse into the film) – Waggett relates an incident indicating his bafflement at how the minds of these Islanders work. Like several of Mrs Campbell's verbal onslaughts, this is taken practically verbatim from the novel, perhaps confirming Mackendrick's remark about bringing Mackenzie back into the scripting process at a late stage and primarily for dialogue:

> 'They're so unsporting. They don't do things for the sake of doing them like the English. We play the game for the sake of the game. Others play the game for the sake of winning it. I tried to introduce football onto the island. I managed to get hold of a football and presented it to the school. I was the referee. I had to give a foul against the Garryboo team. It was more than a foul, it was a deliberate assault. And what do you think happened?'
>
> 'I don't know, sir.'
>
> 'Young Willie Maclellan, the captain of the team, deliberately dribbled the ball to the touchline and kicked it into the sea.'

The meaning of the scene is clearly there in the words, but what gives the scene its force is the sense of incomprehension and incredulity in Radford's playing of it. Elsewhere, Mackendrick has commented on the excellence of Herbert Lom's playing of the gangster Louis in *The Ladykillers* as emanating from Lom's 'acting as if he didn't know he was funny'. Exactly the same can be said of Radford's Waggett. In this sense one might agree with Danischewsky's observation that Mackendrick was becoming increasingly sympathetic to Waggett, but the ending of the film ultimately puts that in doubt. With great narrative economy,

Waggett's conversation with Odd segues into a confrontation between Waggett and Doctor Maclaren (James Robertson Justice) about the roadblock delaying him. Waggett appeals shamelessly to Maclaren's class loyalty to no avail. The two scenes in which Waggett has appeared thus far prepare the audience for the position he will take over the whisky in the wreck.

As has been mentioned, the wreck and the theft of the whisky occur fully halfway into the novel, the first half being taken up principally with the meandering delineation of the diverse 'couthy' characters, a feature which survives in the film mainly in occasional remarks by this or that character. The same events occur just a fifth of the way into the film. The way the news that the wrecked ship is carrying a bonanza of whisky is revealed and transmitted is interestingly different from novel to film. In the novel, some of the ship's crew row ashore and reveal the nature of their cargo almost casually. In the film, the Biffer (Morland Graham) and Sammy MacCodrum (John Gregson) row out and meet the incoming lifeboat. There is a shouted exchange from boat to boat in the course of which the Biffer asks about the cargo. When the answer 'fifty thousand cases of whisky!' is shouted back, the Biffer, in close-up, falls backwards into his boat, the moment being pointed up by heavy musical underlining followed by another close-up of the Biffer repeating trance-like 'fifty thousand cases of whisky'. This scene, virtually identical with the description in the RSS, is immediately followed by one of the film's two virtually wordless montage sequences with the Biffer running around telling everyone about the godsend to the insistent beat of the fastest passages of the film's musical score. There is a note in the RSS that this scene should indeed be a montage sequence and that 'the scenes are accompanied by violent music which has a progression that represents the spreading of glorious news. The images should be shot with something of the same impressionism and the montage should be brisk.' But the very lengthy and more complex montage sequence of the RSS – which includes close-ups of running feet and a repeated musical phrase echoing in its rhythm the words 'fifty thousand cases of whisky' – has given way in the film to a much briefer and more intense montage in line, it would seem, with the major thrust at the post-production stage to soup up the narrative. The transmission of the news is much more casual in the novel, the major focus being the worry expressed by the Protestants of Great Todday that the Catholics of Little Todday will beat them to the wreck because of the onset of the Sabbath. The meandering pace of the novel is entirely transformed in the film as the

Islanders badger the captain of the ferry to set sail, even in the fog, to remove the shipwrecked crew so that they can get to the wreck. Succeeding, they race for their boats and it is only when their enthusiasm is at fever pitch and they are about to embark that the clock sounds the first stroke heralding the arrival of the Sabbath. This is followed by their dejected trudge away from the boats and a brief scene at about eleven in the morning as – several bowler-hatted and all best-suited – they look wistfully at the wreck on their way to church, complaining as they leave church about the length of the minister's sermon. The handling of this event, the building up of enthusiasm followed by a sudden change of mood, reflects the tendency of cinema, as opposed to literature, to structure action in terms of contrasts of mood, alternating swift movement with stasis. It is now that Waggett – his response entirely predictable because of his behaviour in earlier scenes – makes the fateful decision that the Home Guard must take responsibility for guarding the whisky on the wreck until the proper authorities arrive. This scene is, in many respects, the dramatic pivot of the film, what screenwriting manuals call 'the point of no return', and the film's awareness of this is underlined by having Waggett march into a low-angle close-up which emphasizes both the bombast of his stance and the centrality of this moment in the film. His long-suffering wife Dolly – beautifully played by Catherine Lacey – is favoured by a longer than usual close-up which registers her awareness that this 'momentous decision' (the very words used in the RSS) will destroy her husband. There then occurs the brief exchange between Dolly and Waggett which poses the problem at the heart of the film:

> 'Paul … if the salvage people won't touch it, would it be so terrible if the people here did get a few bottles? I mean, if it's all going down to the bottom of the sea … '
>   'That's a very dangerous line of argument, Dolly. Very. Once you let people take the law into their own hands it's anarchy, *anarchy* … '

In fact, these lines, as spoken in the film, are considerably tougher, and cut closer to the heart of the moral issue underpinning the film, than the words Waggett speaks in the RSS, which are: 'That's a very dangerous line of argument, Dolly. Very dangerous. If you start to reason that way there's no knowing where it will end. It is up to people like ourselves to set a standard of behaviour to the others.' Another way of putting this is that the *class* discourse of Waggett's words in the RSS becomes in the film a *political* discourse.

There are a few scenes in *Whisky Galore!* which appear to have no discernible narrative function and which may exist primarily in furtherance of the same impulse of the novel to create 'couthy' characters. However, one such scene – a confrontation between Waggett and Mrs Campbell – is distinguished by the near-surrealist quality of the exchange. Waggett has gone to the Campbell home to speak with George, his second-in-command in the Home Guard, only to be informed by Mrs Campbell that George is locked in his room with bread and cheese and his Bible. In the course of Waggett's expostulations, the following exchange occurs:

'Mrs Campbell, at this very moment our troops are fighting in North Africa. The Germans don't stop fighting on Sundays. How can we?'

'What the Germans do, Mr Waggett, is on their conscience. And Todday is not in North Africa, so there's no need to bring the heathens into it. I'm told there are cannibals in Africa, but no one is going to persuade my son to eat human flesh.'

'No one's *asking* your son to eat human flesh!'

'Not *yet*.'

Surrealistically funny in cold print, it is greatly enhanced by Radford's apoplectic exasperation and Cadell's icy certainty. Although at odds with each other, Waggett and Mrs Campbell are the outsiders in the film, the ones who will not assent to the genial hedonism of whisky and subscribe to its myths. Mrs Campbell will be redeemed back into the community through her consuming of whisky at the *réiteach* – whisky is the magical transformative potion for all the ills in the film. In the novel she simply subsides into a tight-lipped silence. In both novel and film Waggett is cast into outer darkness.

It has been suggested that the three great myths about whisky in Scottish culture relate to bodily health, community and sociability and manhood. It is through whisky that all three are restored in *Whisky Galore!* We had earlier seen the negative side of the bodily health myth in the death of Captain Macphee through want of whisky. After the pillaging of the wreck, we see whisky's positive application in the return to full health of Old Hector (James Anderson), whom we have seen wasting away, after the application of a dram by Doctor Maclaren. The myth of sociability is delivered in the *port a beul* (literally 'mouth music') sequence when the frame is bursting with Islanders all singing in unison and downing large quantities of whisky. This is another example of the film recasting into brief visual and auditory terms what takes up an entire

6a ... *whisky as healthgiving. Doctor Maclaren (James Robertson Justice) rejuvenates old Hector.*

6b ... *whisky as adjunct to sociability. The 'mouth music' scene.*

6. *The three myths of whisky ...*

6c ... *whisky as generator of masculinity. Dr Maclaren gives George the dram that will allow him to face his mother.*

chapter in the novel. The sense of communal joy and increased narrative pace in the *port a beul* sequence is to some extent realized verbally in the novel by the 'torrent' of whisky brand names: 'Besides the famous names known all over the world by ruthless and persistent advertising for many years' (this sentence would come back to haunt Mackenzie in the light of his own later contract to advertise Grant's 'Standfast') 'there were many blends of the finest quality, less famous, perhaps, but not less delicious. There were Highland Gold and Highland Heart, Tartan Milk and Tartan Perfection, Bluebell, Northern Light, Prestonpans, Queen of the Glens ... ' The list goes on for forty-three brands, then the pace quickens: 'There were spherical bottles and dimpled bottles and square bottles and oblong bottles and flagon-shaped bottles and high-waisted bottles and ordinary bottles.'[6] It is instructive to note how novel and film deploy different strategies to signify rising excitement.

The *port a beul* sequence in the film was one of the late additions, incorporated under Charles Crichton's re-editing at Ealing Studios and actually shot there using local actors and a handful of actors from the film. It very clearly has a 'wild' soundtrack which does not match the

mouth movements of the actors and is one of the scenes which gives
Whisky Galore! a kind of Frankenstein-monster quality – made up of
bits and pieces from here and there – which has tended to be overlooked
on account of the affection the film has inspired and through the logic
of certain critical paradigms. For instance, any auteurist account of
Whisky Galore! will tend to homogenize everything in it under the sway
of Mackendrick.

The other central myth about whisky in the film – its relationship to
manhood – is delivered by way of George's emancipation from his
mother's tyranny. Again, this occupies a lengthy chapter in the novel
and, like the book as a whole and *unlike* the film, is very desultory.
George's 'victory' is wholly at the level of the word. Mrs Campbell
wilts under his whisky-fuelled verbal assault:

> 'If I make a cup of tea, George, will you not open a bottle of the liquor?'
>   'As long as I have something to drink I don't mind,' he answered and
> almost chuckled aloud, for this was the first time his mother had ever
> bargained with him. He knew now that she was beaten before the battle
> began.[7]

Once more in the film this wholly verbal discourse is rendered into
action. Primed by Doctor Maclaren with several drams, George returns
to his mother's house and, faced with another incipient tirade, does not
shout his mother down but, taking his father's bagpipes which have
framed his father's photograph on the wall, *plays* his mother into silence.
It scarcely needs to be pointed out how resoundingly patriarchal this
resolution is. It is constructed as whisky giving a man the courage to
take up his legitimate patriarchal inheritance and lay down the law in his
own house. This book began by referring to the unconscious discourses
within which *Whisky Galore!* and *The Maggie* were constructed, patriarchy being one of them. This sequence shows unconscious patriarchy
at its most rampant. Quite unambiguously, the film asks us to approve
of what it considers the restitution of the 'natural' state of affairs in the
Campbell household. The Introduction also speaks of gaps and fissures
in the unconscious discourses. In relation to patriarchy there is a price
to be paid, as the ending of the film will reveal.

Whisky Galore! is constructed within the norms of classic cinematic
narrative. With the *port a beul* sequence celebrating the haul of whisky
and George's successful showdown with his mother, the film has reached
its high-water mark. The Islanders are decidedly in the ascendant. The
classic narrative form decrees, therefore, that there must be a dramatic

reversal. This is delivered in Waggett's summoning the Customs and Excise officers who arrive to the tune of the Robert Burns song 'The Deil's Awa' wi' the Exciseman'. The film sustains the dramatic reversal by intercutting the arrival of the excisemen with the *réiteach* at which the Islanders enjoy a foursome reel danced by the two engaged couples. Philip Kemp has fruitfully compared *Whisky Galore!* with the war movie genre – there is even a 'quisling' in the shape of the owner of the bar whose trade is ruined by the free whisky from the wreck – and this is particularly true of the representation of Farquarson (Henry Mollison) and his excisemen. Dressed in black, they resemble nothing so much as a squad of SS or Gestapo men walking the Todday street and fanning out to do a house-to-house search for the whisky. Indeed, as they leave their cutter, the lighting makes their oilskins look like leather coats. The 'war movie' look is, of course, enhanced by the scenes of Home Guard activity imported from *Keep the Home Guard Turning*. As conceived in the RSS, and as played by Mollison, Farquarson is a sardonic realist, half enjoying the laugh the Islanders are having at his expense and openly contemptuous of Waggett. Paring his nails with a little pair of scissors, which he hands to Waggett when the latter observes that they will have to cut themselves out of the barbed wire in which the Islanders have enmeshed their car, Farquarson is reminiscent of those SS officers in wartime movies who play the piano while interrogating their prisoners.

The arrival of the excisemen provokes what has become the most famous sequence in *Whisky Galore!* – the hiding of the whisky, the second of the (virtually) wordless montages which has been described by Murray Grigor as 'Mackendrick's answer to anyone who says that story-boards are redundant'. The problem with this judgement is that there is some doubt whether Mackendrick was actually responsible for the sequence. For instance, it is absent from the RSS which carries a more extended search sequence involving individual excise officers searching particular crofts and houses. This survives in the film in the very brief sequence of Islanders hiding bottles in the guttering of a house, Sammy MacCodrum attempting to conceal bottles in rabbit holes and finding them 'occupied' and Angus MacCormac (Duncan Macrae) rescuing the dregs of two bottles of whisky which his mother has been emptying down the sink. This sequence looks as though it ought to be part of the 'new' rapid montage, but it is separated from it by the very quiet scene of Farquarson's visit to Macroon. The 'missing' rapid montage sequence is in the post-production script (also held by the British Film Institute) and in the film, as follows:

(M = MEDIUM, C = CLOSE, L = LONG)
MLS   excisemen outside house
CS   bottles
MS   bottles and milk cans
MCS   stove
MCS   hot-water bottles
MCS   man and lamp
MS   pie dish
MCS   file
MS   drain
MS   grandfather clock
MS   violin case
MCS   money till
MS   grandfather clock
MCS   violin case
MCS   money till
MS   baby in cradle.

All these objects are places in which the whisky bottles are hidden in this extremely rapid montage. The repetition of the grandfather clock, violin and money till at the end reflects their being first opened and then closed with the whisky inside them. The sequence, which lasts only seconds, is accompanied by very brisk music. Given what we know about *Whisky Galore!* being cut and recut, this seems like exactly the kind of sequence which Charles Crichton might have shot in Ealing and added to the final edit. There is nothing in any of the individual images which ties them to any member of the cast. Apart from the baby in the final image, all the audience sees are hands and bottles. It should be recalled, however, that Crichton claims to have liaised with Mackendrick on the final edit.

And so to the ending of *Whisky Galore!* As set out in the RSS, the ending overlaps with that of the film as we have it, but is altogether more low-key, closing on the reverse of the aerial sequence with which the RSS opens, so that the plane flies away from Todday. Also in the RSS is a version of the moralizing ending which Danischewsky says he added since 'we were anxious not to offend the moralists'. The RSS runs:

COMMENTARY
... but the price of whisky went up ... and then it went up again ... until nobody in Todday could afford a wee dram. So we all lived unhappily ever after. Except Odd and Peggy and George and Catriona.

For they were not whisky drinkers. And if that isn't a moral story – what is?

This is substantially as we have it in the film, except that – against a reprise of Odd and Peggy walking on the beach – the reference in the commentary is to them alone, possibly because including George would be at odds with what whisky has done for him in the film. There are two particularly interesting changes from the RSS to the finished film. Waggett has, of course, been hoist by his own petard. The ammunition boxes he sent off the island, under his own signature, have been found to contain six bottles of illicit whisky from the wreck. He is therefore taken away from Todday to be questioned by the Excise, presented in both RSS and film as his effectively being driven out of the community. However, missing from the film is the sharp irony in the RSS whereby, as the ferry draws away from Todday with Waggett slumped disconsolately on the rail looking back at the island he has been driven from, he looks down into the water and sees floating there an empty whisky bottle. This omission from the film as we have it is puzzling, given the emphasis Mackendrick placed on dramatic irony, to the extent of producing a handout devoted to the topic when he taught film at the California Institute of Arts. However, the strangest and most resonant change from RSS to film concerns Dolly Waggett's response to her husband's destruction. In the RSS, as Waggett sits stupefied by the defeat he has suffered at the hands of the Islanders, Farquarson receives the telephone call – the content of which he imparts to Waggett with some relish – about the whisky in the ammunition boxes. Dolly's response in the RSS is verbal and low-key:

> DOLLY (in a desperately artless manner): Really, Paul dear – don't you think you've rather been running with the hare and hunting with the hounds?

Her response in the film is altogether more chilling and unsettling. She begins to laugh, and laugh, and laugh and, as her laughter reaches hysterical proportions, Waggett's horror-stricken face gives way (and here there is a resonant sound dissolve as well) to a reprise of the dance sequence from the *réiteach*. Dolly's demented laughter remains for some time on the soundtrack over the laughing faces of the Islanders, creating the impression that they too are laughing at Waggett – his humiliation and exclusion are now total – before dissolving into the sounds of the dance. This electrifying change from RSS to film throws up two interesting critical questions. Part of this book's argument is that *Whisky Galore!* as both novel and film is constructed within an unconscious patriarchal discourse rendered not only in the predominantly male production ethos, but the whole conception of the project, and delivered most 'purely' and least consciously in the sequence of George's triumph over his mother. The Waggett/Dolly relationship is also constructed patriarchally, but here the discourse begins to seep to the surface, to become almost conscious. A key dimension of Waggett's being constructed as arrogant and stiff-necked is his supercilious and condescending attitude to Dolly. That is, at some level the writers/director of *Whisky Galore!* recognize that there is something *wrong* with this relationship, although they probably saw the problem as being a flaw in Waggett's character rather than a symptom of the more general question of patriarchy. Read with this in mind, Dolly's laughter becomes not simply the reaction of a woman to the downfall of an individually callous spouse, but quite precisely a *hysterical* response to a profoundly unconscious and naturalized patriarchal discourse which neither the character nor the makers of the film have the analytical apparatus to discern but which nevertheless blights her life. This is conveyed not simply by the fact of Dolly's laughter, but by its *degree*. That is, the film is here displaying artistic excess, an intensity of realization greater than the event being depicted warrants – a sure sign of the film being troubled at this stage by the discourse it is itself constructed within. It was suggested above that the omission of the floating whisky bottle was curious, given Mackendrick's fondness for dramatic irony. Perhaps the irony is being expressed – at a conscious level – in Dolly's laughter, which is very reminiscent of the demented laughter that suffuses the soundtrack at the end of *The Treasure of the Sierra Madre* – widely discussed in the late 1940s in the context of dramatic irony – as the gold dust, which the protagonists have been prepared to kill for, is scattered by the wind.

The intensity of Waggett's humiliation and destruction, its delirious realization at the level of the *mise-en-scène*, throws considerable doubt on the oft-relayed view that Mackendrick was sympathetic to Waggett. How, it might be asked, could anyone sympathetic to this character fashion his destruction with such evident relish, inviting the audience to savour every detail. This is precisely the question which must be directed to the, if this is possible, even greater humiliation of Calvin B. Marshall in *The Maggie*. On the other hand, as the production history of *Whisky Galore!* might suggest, perhaps the ending was out of Mackendrick's hands.

The background to the credits of *The Maggie* is an initial image of a map of Scotland followed by a series of marine charts of the River Clyde and its estuary with a whisky glass, a curved pipe and a model of a puffer. A puffer is the generic name for the kind of vessel 'The Maggie' is, a small cargo boat plying the coastal trade in the archipelago that stretches north and south from the mouth of the Clyde. After the initial shot, only the model puffer is shown, to the effect that the actual voyage of the puffer in the film is foreshadowed in the credits. As with *Whisky Galore!*, the credits tell the audience about the geographical location and, as previously, are accompanied by the kind of bouncy music announcing a comedy. There is a certain continuity between the music of the two films. Although credited to different composers – Ernest Irving in the case of *Whisky Galore!* and John Addison in the case of *The Maggie* – they are both played by the Philharmonia Orchestra. It was suggested in the discussion of *Whisky Galore!* that the presence of a classical orchestra on the soundtrack – particularly one, as in the case of *Whisky Galore!*, playing folk airs – represents the unconscious intrusion into the film of the class discourse within which the Ealing team lived. This is still present, though with a difference, in *The Maggie*. The main musical theme, played aggressively by the full classical orchestra, engages in a kind of dialectic with the same theme, played much less aggressively on a concertina. At one level, it has the function of an overture, fore-shadowing in musical language the central dramatic conflict of the film between Calvin B. Marshall, the brash, bustling American airline executive, and Captain Mactaggart, the Scottish master of 'The Maggie'. However, it is also worth noting that the concertina – which is at one stage played on screen by Hamish the Mate – is, in class terms, a more appropriate instrument for the milieu depicted. As Philip Kemp notes:

> Midway through the credits … John Addison's score takes an unexpected turn, modulating into something altogether more ominous: a mournful horn motif leading – as Mackendrick's credit appears – into a descending string glissando rounded off by solemn chords in the bass. This, the score seems to imply, will be a comedy with very dark undertones – or alternatively, a fairly schizophrenic movie. Or, as it turns out, both.[8]

One could go further and claim that this is certainly Mackendrick's most bleak and cruel comedy, perhaps his most bleak and cruel film. However, the evidence for that will be delivered much later in the film. The tone at the beginning is very light and comic, even though the first scene after the credits sounds another ominous note. 'The Maggie' is seen coming up the Clyde into Glasgow and being spotted by two harbour officials, one of whom asks if Mactaggart is 'the one that had that trouble in the Kyles'. His companion, reaching for the phone, indicates that Mactaggart 'is asking for it this time'. The next shot shows the crew of 'The Maggie', the Engineman (Abe Barker) berating Mactaggart (Alex Mackenzie) for having put into Glasgow in broad daylight and being reassured that no one would believe them to have the effrontery to do so. In short, it is made clear, right from the start, that Mactaggart and his crew are a source of trouble.

The two major commentators on *The Maggie*, Charles Barr and Philip Kemp, both find it an ultimately unsatisfactory film. Their reasons will be addressed more fully below, but one of the benefits of considering *Whisky Galore!* and *The Maggie* together is that it throws into relief Mackendrick's remarkable development, in the half decade or so between the films, as a *metteur-en-scène*, as an organizer and choreographer of figures and movement within the frame. Glimpsed only intermittently in *Whisky Galore!*, what we see fully developed in *The Maggie* is an often formally complex, yet always narratively economical, *mise-en-scène*. The shooting script of *The Maggie* held by the British Film Institute is dated 22 May 1953 and is headed FIRST SHOOTING SCRIPT (hereafter FSS) and bears a note that: 'This is not a FINAL SHOOTING SCRIPT. A few scenes on which further background work and research must be done, are not broken down.'

However, there is little indication in this script of the ambitiousness of the *mise-en-scène*. This is exemplified at a relatively simple level in the way the crew of 'The Maggie' are introduced. There is a mid-shot of the vessel docked in Glasgow, and the crew enter the shot one by one, clambering up a ladder, first Mactaggart, then the Engineman, then the Mate (James Copeland). Mactaggart, in the course of his argument with the Engineman, informs us that he is 'still master of this vessel'. By the end of this shot the three are lined up on the quayside. This leaves only one other member of the crew to be introduced, Douggie, the Wee Boy, and this is achieved by having the three adult members of the crew and look down into 'The Maggie' where the Wee Boy is working. That is, by two quite simple camera set-ups and the thoughtful movement of figures, the whole crew is introduced. The strategy followed throughout the film is to shoot the four crew members, where this is not narratively impermissible, together within the frame. This is not unconnected with the values they are meant to represent – communitarian rather than individualistic – in the dramatic oppositions of the film,

7. *Communitarian framing. The crew of* The Maggie, *from left to right,
Douggie (Tommy Kearins), Mactaggart (Alex Mackenzie),
the Engineman (Abe Barker) and the Mate (James Copeland).*

even if they often behave like ferrets in a sack in their relationships with
each other. Mactaggart and the Engineman, in particular, are always at
each other's throats. As the three adults depart for the pub, there are two
further brief scenes structured to be in dramatic conflict with each other.
Instructed by Mactaggart to perform certain tasks, Douggie instead

enters the wheelhouse of the boat and, to a wistful version of the main musical theme, strokes the wheel. This is an important little scene, signifying as it does Douggie's mystical attachment to 'The Maggie'. It is he who will be its most passionate advocate and, ultimately, agent of its redemption. His reverie is interrupted by the arrival of two harbour inspectors intent on revoking the boat's loading licence. It is clear that Mackendrick/Rose's research regarding the port of Glasgow was good. Like the fragile Englishman, Pusey (Hubert Gregg), Marshall's assistant, the two harbour inspectors wear bowler hats. But whereas Pusey's bowler (described in the FSS as a 'homburg') signifies his wimpish qualities, those of the harbour inspectors signify the harsh hierarchic regime of the Glasgow docks and shipyards in which figures in direct authority, such as foremen and inspectors, invariably wore bowler hats as a sign of their status. It also signifies class aspirations in the Glasgow docks context as in Gordon Jackson's adopting a bowler when he is elevated from shop floor to drawing office in *Floodtide*.

Mackendrick's *mise-en-scène* is rarely as visceral as that of, say, Nicholas Ray or Vincente Minnelli, but it is equally interesting and complex. This is shown to great effect in the pub scene which immediately follows the arrival of the inspectors, a scene which, like the two which precede it, is structured round a dramatic reversal. Mactaggart is holding forth, with not a little portentousness and in the face of considerable derision, about the freedom he enjoys as an independent operator, chiding the other seamen present that they lack 'the dignity of your own command'. Shown in the FSS as *nine* separate shots, the film as shot delivers a two-and-a-half-minute continuous shot – interrupted by two brief cutaways to the barman – in which several complex actions are realized, obviously requiring considerable planning with regard to the movement of camera and actors. From a mid-shot of Mactaggart in full flow, Mackendrick follows the movement of the barman – following the movement of an object or person masks the fact that the camera is moving – through the crowd to reveal that Hamish the Mate is in the snug making up to a barmaid. He then follows the movement of another actor to bring the camera back on to Mactaggart and moves into close-up on him as he reaches the climax of his peroration, which has been going on throughout: 'As for my boat, there's not a finer vessel in the coastal trade. There's not a finer vessel anywhere. There's ... there's ...' At this point Douggie slips under Mactaggart's gesticulating arm with, 'There's two men on board us – with bowler hats!'

The same single shot then allows the Engineman to fetch Hamish from the snug before picking up Mactaggart again and tracking forwards with him as he makes for the door with Douggie. The film then initiates what is to become something of a running gag – payments of any kind being unloaded on to the Wee Boy. With Mactaggart gone to confront the inspectors, the camera – still, it will be recalled, within the same complex set of movements – tracks backwards with Douggie as he approaches the bar to pay Mactaggart's tab, then he himself becomes the centre of further action in an assault upon one of the derisive customers who has insulted Mactaggart. The camera then tracks forward with Douggie, his collar firmly gripped by the barman, until he is ejected from the bar when a further dramatic reversal occurs as the barman, crowing in the doorway, is hit in the face by a missile directed by the now off-camera Douggie. It is suggested that all of these complex movements are executed within a single two-and-a-half-minute shot punctuated by two cutaways. It seems certainly to have been planned that way, although the cutaways (though narratively entirely appropriate) may have been inserted to conceal the fact that parts of more than one take were used. Nevertheless, the argument certainly holds good for about the first two minutes of the shot, eloquent testimony to the sophistication of *mise-en-scène* Mackendrick had achieved by this stage in his career. If external confirmation is required, there are the remarks of Burt Lancaster about shooting *Sweet Smell of Success* with Mackendrick:

> He'd set up shots on the sound stage for a scene that would play six minutes … There would be thirty-five camera moves on a dolly. The whole floor was taped. We had to hit marks like crazy. The camera moved continuously – into close-ups, pulling back, shooting over here to this person … We rehearsed all day, until four in the afternoon just to get the technical part down. The head grip and the rest of the crew were sweating, knowing that if they missed one mark the shot would be ruined. But we did it, clicked it all off.[9]

The key point, however, is that, complex though these multiple movements of camera and actors are, they are never complex for their own sake, never flashy or self-advertising, but *always* at the service of clarity and economy of storytelling.

Central to this book is the argument that both *Whisky Galore!* and *The Maggie* partake unconsciously of powerful narratives at play in British culture at the time the films were made (and, indeed, still at play), narratives relating to class, gender and ethnicity although, as has been suggested, the films' relationship to these narratives may sometimes be complex, oblique and contradictory. However, there are two other strong narratives *The Maggie* might have surrendered to, but did not: those relating to Glasgow and to childhood. *The Maggie* is one of the few movies that deal with both rural, Highland, Gaelic-speaking Scotland and urban, Lowland, English-speaking Scotland. *Floodtide* is another film that incorporates the rural/urban opposition, but the rural element in that film is also Lowland and English-speaking. Glasgow, the city in which *The Maggie* begins and ends, has generated a particularly powerful narrative which might be called Glasgow as City of Dreadful Night. So dominant has this narrative been – it is now to some extent being challenged by two more recently manufactured myths about Glasgow: the city of culture and the city of urban chic – that it is surprising to learn that, in the eighteenth century, Glasgow was most often bracketed with Oxford on account of the quality of its air and the beauty of its ambience. The rot set in with the Industrial Revolution after which social surveys, prints, photographs, novels, paintings, poetry, tabloid journalism, films and television plays and documentaries have constructed Glasgow as the City of Dreadful Night within which morose, sectarian, razor-scarred men stalk the worst slums in Europe, consigning their womenfolk (always represented as mothers or lovers, never as autonomous subjects) to the margins of experience. This, then, was the dominant narrative of Glasgow when *The Maggie* was being made in the early 1950s and which would have beckoned the filmmakers in relation to the early scenes set there. It is to their credit that they did not succumb to it (even if the scene outside the pub in which Mactaggart, Hamish the Mate and the Engineman have just drunk the £50 they have conned out of Pusey, has echoes of the bleak pub scenes in *The Gorbals Story*), rather using Glasgow as the harshly hierarchical and repressive Other to the film's imagined warm and communitarian Highland society through which 'The Maggie' sails. That said, as will be argued below, one has to be much more censorious about the apparently beneficent way the film constructs Highland society.

Just as there are dominant narratives about Scotland and Glasgow, so too is there a dominant narrative about childhood within which the child is seen as innately innocent, placid, asexual and 'nice'. There is, of course, an equally reductive counter-narrative of the innately evil child. The cinema has partaken of both, with particularly dire consequences regarding the dominant myth, as a glance at the history of child stars from Shirley Temple, through Margaret O'Brien to Macaulay Culkin will testify. However, certain filmmakers – for example, Vincente Minnelli with Margaret O'Brien in *Meet Me in St Louis* or Victor Erice with the child actors in *Spirit of the Beehive* – have managed to construct a more complex view of childhood that is perhaps more often encountered in literature such as Henry James's *The Turn of the Screw* or Angela Carter's *The Company of Wolves*. Alexander Mackendrick undoubtedly falls into this latter category, as his work in *Mandy*, *Sammy Going South*, *A High Wind in Jamaica* and, of course, *The Maggie* demonstrates. With regard to the dominant narrative of childhood, the gaping trap that awaits any filmmaker is sentimentality. One would be very hard-pressed to find any trace of this in the construction of Douggie: no 'tear-jerking' scenes, no lingering close-ups, no smart-arsed ripostes, not a hint of 'the cutes'. Douggie's role in the film is crucial, but it hinges on his intelligence as a character, not on his 'innate' appeal as a child. The dignity and restraint of what *The Maggie* asks of its child actor may be contrasted with that of a more recent film, *Leon*, which achieves the difficult feat of being simultaneously sentimental and prurient with regard to its child actor, Nathalie Portman. The question of Mackendrick's control of senti- mentality could be directed to the adult performances too. Consider, for example, James Copeland's restrained, monosyllabic Hamish with his appallingly sentimental performance, as the kind of 'professional Scots- man' Alastair Sim despised, in *Innocents in Paris*. There is one scene in *The Maggie*, however, over which critics have accused Mackendrick of just this kind of loss of control. There is, indeed, loss of control in this scene, but it will be argued that the loss of control is not psychological, but ideological.

The fateful confusion – the 'inciting incident' as the screenwriting manuals would call it – which sets the plot in motion, occurs at the office of Mr Campbell (Geoffrey Keen), the shipping agent to whom the crew of 'The Maggie' have gone in the vain hope of selling him a £300 share in their boat which will allow them to repair its plates and have its loading licence renewed. Having informed Pusey that there is no boat available to take Marshall's cargo to the Islands, Campbell rushes off, leaving Mactaggart to inform Pusey – engaged in one of his interminable phone calls to Marshall – that he has a boat. This sequence throws up a number of interesting points about Mackendrick's control of *mise-en-scène* and the extent to which *The Maggie* partakes of unconscious discourse, this time of *class*. What is particularly bold about the *mise-en-scène* is the number of planes of action it encompasses within the single shot. If the earlier scene in the pub was stylistically reminiscent of Max

Ophuls, this sequence is reminiscent of the cinema of Orson Welles (whose work Mackendrick greatly admired to the extent of drawing many of his teaching examples at Cal-Arts from Welles's films). The sequence several times incorporates five planes of action and, on occasion, *seven*. As with the pub sequence, there is the same preference for the long take, rather than the shot/counter-shot, with the actors moving in and out of the frame and, on occasion – as in the culmination of Pusey's telephone conversation with Marshall – focus-pulling being used to isolate Pusey within the frame. But even here, although Mactaggart is in the out-of-focus background and therefore does not invite our gaze, Mackendrick has him turn his back to the camera to ensure that nothing distracts our attention from Pusey's telephone conversation with Marshall in which is revealed the important information that Pusey must check out the sea-worthiness of Mactaggart's boat (a previous telephone conversation has revealed the equally important plot element that the cargo must be insured for £4,000). Once again, Mackendrick's formally rich *mise-en-scène* is entirely at the service of narrative clarity.

The point to be made about Geoffrey Keen's performance is similar to that already made about Joan Greenwood's in *Whisky Galore!* – the intrusion of middle-class English theatrical intonation into the playing of a petty-bourgeois Scottish character. The issue is pointed up by Hubert Gregg's role and performance in the same sequence. Gregg's role, as written and performed, is a consciously satirical representation of a certain type of middle-class Englishman. That is, the film *knows* what it is doing *vis-à-vis* the Gregg role. My contention is that it does *not* know what it is doing in the case of the Keen performance. Keen's class formation – he was a classically trained Shakespearean actor on the London stage and the son of the distinguished Shakespearean actor Malcolm Keen – seeps unconsciously, principally through his voice production and cadences, into his performance as Campbell. Once more, the unconscious class discourse has insinuated its way into the film. A similar point could be made about the performance of Andrew Keir, who plays the reporter Fraser. This time the argument would be about a Scot being deracinated, in terms of voice quality and body language, by professional theatrical training and the (metropolitan English) norms of the Scottish theatre at this time.

There are, from time to time in the FSS, some indications of how the *mise-en-scène* of particular scenes will operate. Such is the case with the scene in which Pusey goes to inspect the vessel he has just chartered and, arriving on the quayside, assumes that the large, sparkling cargo ship moored alongside the tiny puffer is the vessel he is looking for. The scene is set out in the FSS as follows:

EXT, GLASGOW DOCKS. L.S. DAY

CAMERA shoots towards the place where the wooden ladder reaches the top of the wharf. Being at a distance from the edge, we can see nothing of 'The Maggie' except the top of the derrick. PUSEY is walking diagonally across picture. Belatedly, as he reaches the edge of the frame, the CAMERA PANS slowly with him, thus explaining his error [in confusing the boats]. The movement introduces the stern of the big cargo vessel berthed beside the puffer. The SKIPPER [Mactaggart] enters from behind the camera.

There is a Hitchcockian element introduced to both script and film. As Mactaggart signs the contract with Pusey, an officer of the larger vessel looks on suspiciously (from the deck in the script and from the quayside in the film), setting up a tension between Mactaggart's signing the contract and his discomfort at being watched doing something underhand or, perhaps, his unease that the watching officer will give the game away.

As has been suggested, the film's view of Douggie is clear-eyed and unsentimental, investing him with considerable nous and force of character that make his criminal acts – such as stealing Campbell's fountain pen and poaching grouse – dramatically if not morally acceptable. When 'The Maggie' does set sail with the three drunken adults in control, it is Douggie who, thanklessly, warns them of the tide conditions that will lead to the boat being grounded on the Glasgow underground's metal air-vent protruding from the river, thus making Mactaggart and the puffer once more a laughing stock. A crowd gathers to jeer and one wag calls Mactaggart 'Captain Carlsen', a reference to a popular hero of 1952. Captain Henrik Carlsen, his ship having run aground off the Cornish coast, ordered his crew and passengers to safety but remained on board himself for twelve days until heavy seas dragged his vessel down. This no longer decipherable reference (except to those who read newspapers or heard news bulletins in the early 1950s) should alert us to the wider possibility that our reading of films may change over time. There follows a series of scenes which are very dense in information-giving terms (much of it imparted by telephone) and in which several characters not previously seen – including Marshall himself – make their first appearance. Having only heard his voice on the telephone, we first see Marshall in his plush London offices with a map of the world covering one wall and a model of a plane in flight on his desk. He is questioning the wretched Pusey as a disembodied, off-camera voice:

PUSEY: ... and he ... he gave me ... his *signature*!
MARSHALL: Well?
PUSEY: He signed the inventory!
MARSHALL: So?
PUSEY: So naturally I ... I chartered the boat.
MARSHALL: And?

It is only after this conversation that we actually see Marshall behind his desk. The question he then asks hints at the degree of disorientation which will eventually engulf him:

MARSHALL: Just let me get one thing straight. Are you saying a boat is stuck on a subway?

Mackendrick – through his complex *mise-en-scène* and deep focus involving several planes of action – partially solves the narrative problem of the information-giving scenes involved in Marshall's visit to Glasgow by having much of it happen simultaneously. This also increases the comic effect by creating something close to bedlam round the unfortunate Marshall who has come to Glasgow confident that his drive and authority will iron out the problem 'in an hour'. In one scene he has invited Campbell to his hotel suite to help him retrieve his cargo from 'The Maggie', only to have Mactaggart's sister Sarah – somewhat in the mould of 'Mistress' Campbell from *Whisky Galore!* – burst in to demand the money she feels she is owed, under the impression that the boat, of which she is part-owner, has been sold to Marshall. In the FSS, Sarah is introduced much earlier and has a long scene with Mactaggart which fills out the nature of their relationship and seems designed primarily to demonstrate Mactaggart's low cunning, as in his flattery of Sarah: 'Ye're no' so copious aboot the body as when I last saw ye. It becomes ye.'

In this scene, Mactaggart seems written to be played as a Lowland Scot, but Alex Mackenzie plays the character as Highland and Gaelic-speaking, although the other members of the crew are played Glaswegian. There is no dramatic reason for Mactaggart to be played Highland but, as will be seen, there is a profound *ideological* reason. The scene in the film in which Sarah is introduced is 'bedlamized' by having Pusey, Marshall's secretary, a hotel waiter and a local reporter swirl in the background. What we see here for the first time is a situation which Marshall is unused to and which will grow in intensity as the film progresses – his diminishing capacity to dominate events. The FSS's directions to the actor are quite explicit about Marshall's loosening grip – 'he is beginning to be uneasy', 'he is increasingly concerned', 'dismayed', 'remonstrating', 'appalled'. Mackendrick apparently was unhappy with Paul Douglas's playing of Marshall:

> I wanted him to be thoroughly nasty, a real hard, vicious executive brute, up to the point where he begins to come unstuck. And then you'd feel a warming and a softening of the character. But Paul wouldn't play nasty, because he felt insecure; he knew instinctively he was being acted off the screen by Alex Mackenzie and the wee boy, and maybe he didn't trust his director.[10]

Mackendrick's point is difficult to understand. Perhaps he did not get quite the performance he wanted from Douglas, but maybe we should trust the tale and not the artist here. Douglas's physical bulk and morose demeanour seem to me to bring an entirely adequate 'heaviness' to the role, bearing in mind the prejudices a British audience would have had at that time about an American 'lording it' in the UK.

During Marshall's stay in Glasgow, the film initiates a sub-plot which will appear intermittently throughout – Marshall's telephone calls to his wife apologizing for his work keeping him away from her and hinting that all is not well between them. It will be recalled that William Rose had written out of the script the actual appearance of Marshall's wife, one of the factors Mackendrick blamed for the film's mediocre box-office performance. Watching this first telephone call, the question that immediately springs to the viewer's mind is why is Marshall, and the room in which he makes the call, lit as sombrely as the most bleak American film noir, the great initial cycle of which would come to an end a few years later with Orson Welles's *Touch of Evil*? There is some evidence that this scene – and indeed the whole sub-plot about the absent wife – touched Mackendrick personally:

> [*The Maggie*] is dealing with problems private to Mackendrick, and of little relevance to the rest of the world, and that's probably what's wrong with it … It's the most self-indulgent of my films, in that it's the most personal and the most private. It came at a difficult time, because Hilary and I were having marital problems, which is reflected in some of the writing. All the principal characters are me in a way.[11]

The comments might well apply to this scene but, as will be argued presently, there is a more fundamental reading of Mackendrick's remarks. Although an explanation of this order might be offered for the 'noirish' lighting of this particular scene, the same kind of lighting occurs in two later scenes – one involving Marshall and Fraser, the other Pusey and Campbell – to which this explanation is not applicable. It will be recalled that, in Mackendrick's remarks on the writing of *The Maggie* cited earlier, he puts the lack of popular success of the film down to Rose's excision of the onscreen presence of Marshall's wife. Mackendrick is here articulating another barely conscious ideology relating to 'Hollywoodian' cinema – the absolute centrality of heterosexual romance. Virginia Wright Wexman begins her book *Creating the Couple: Love, Marriage and Hollywood Performance* with these words:

> In their monumental study *The Classical Hollywood Cinema*, David Bordwell, Janet Staiger, and Kristin Thompson have calculated that 85 per cent of all Hollywood films made before 1960 have romance as their main plot, and 95 per cent have romance as either the main plot or a secondary plot. This empirical data corroborates a commonly held perception: in most Hollywood films, romantic love is a major concern. As in contemporary American culture generally, romantic love in Hollywood has traditionally been seen as properly culminating in marriage; thus, these movies are overwhelmingly preoccupied with what received Hollywood wisdom knows as its most reliable formula: boy meets girl, boy loses girl, boy gets girl. Raymond Bellour has called this convention 'the creation of the couple' and has identified it as a pattern that 'organizes, indeed constitutes, the classical American cinema as a whole.'[12]

As we have seen, heterosexual romance culminating in (projected) marriage is ostensibly central to *Whisky Galore!* (although Mackendrick's real interests may have centred the film on other concerns). It is present also in *The Maggie*, but in a displaced form (in the Sheena episode, to be discussed presently) and in a repressed form (the Marshall/Mrs Marshall relationship). However, it is no more clear if its relative absence from *The Maggie* was the key reason for that film's lack of critical and commercial success, than if its (ostensible) presence in *Whisky Galore!* was central to its warm reception.

The Maggie is a much more intricately constructed film than *Whisky Galore!* The central dramatic opposition between Marshall and Mactaggart has the quality of a fencing match, first one then the other appearing to have the advantage. It would seem, from the FSS, that the process of rewriting the script was a continuous one, pushing right into the shooting script stage – again, not an unusual practice in the film industry. Some of this can be gathered from the FSS by the introduction of new pages from time to time. Such a set of page insertions – headed NEW 54, NEW NEW 55 and NEW 55A – deliver one of the joys of the film which encapsulates the (to change the metaphor) poker-playing relationship between Marshall and Mactaggart. Forced to track the runaway puffer by chartered aircraft, Marshall catches sight of it in the sea below:

MARSHALL: Where do you reckon they're making for?
PILOT: It looks like they're putting into Inverkerran for the night.

Marshall looks down at the puffer with a poker player's speculativeness.

MARSHALL: Tell me, if *they* thought I thought they were going to Inverkerran, where do you reckon they would make for *then*?
PILOT: Strathcathaig, maybe.
MARSHALL (frowning, looking down): This sounds silly, but if they thought I'd think they were going to Strathcathaig because it looked as if they were going to Inverkerran – where would they go then?
PILOT: My guess would be Pennymaddy.
MARSHALL: If there's such a thing as a triple bluff, I bet Mactaggart invented it. Okay, Pennymaddy.

This is followed immediately by a shot of the crew of the puffer looking upwards at the plane, a scene in which (to change the game metaphor yet again) Mactaggart makes a series of pre-emptive chess moves.

MACTAGGART: Aye, he'll have guessed we're making for Inverkerran.
HAMISH: Will he not go there himself, then?
MACTAGGART: Oh, no. He'll know we know he's seen us, so he'll be expecting us to head for Strathcathaig instead.
HAMISH: Will I set her for Pennymaddy, then?
MACTAGGART: No. If it should occur to him that it's occurred to us that he's expecting us to go to Strathcathaig, he would think we'll be making for Pennymaddy.
HAMISH: Well, then, shall I set her for Penwhannoy?
MACTAGGART: No. We'll make for Inverkerran just as we planned. It's the last thing he's likely to think of.

However, it is part of the overall dramatic structure of the film that control shifts back and forth between the two characters. The above scene, with Mactaggart in control, is reversed in a briefer scene in which, Marshall now aboard the puffer, Mactaggart and the Engineman plot to sabotage the engine to prevent the boat getting to the place where Marshall intends to switch his cargo to another vessel. Marshall informs them that, should they be thinking about doing anything to the engine, he had built a better one when he was eight years old.

We have spoken of the intricacy of the film's construction, but that very intricacy creates a dramaturgical problem which Mackendrick/Rose solve brilliantly. So rapid is the dramatic give and take between Marshall and Mactaggart that the film is in danger of reaching its climax – the destruction of Marshall – too early. This problem is solved by halting temporarily the escalating disintegration of Marshall and transferring it to Pusey, thereby foreshadowing Marshall's fall without visiting it on him too early in the film. Marshall has caught up with the puffer and had his first face-to-face confrontation with Mactaggart. Mackendrick's remarks about the inadequacy of Douglas's performance are certainly not borne out by the viciousness with which he turns on Mactaggart: 'if you want to know the real reason I'm taking this cargo away from you, it's simply that <u>nobody ever gets away with trying to make a monkey out of me</u>' (underlining in the FSS).

Marshall puts Pusey on to the puffer to ensure that it discharges his cargo at the next port, but it is like delivering a lamb into the wolves' lair. Caught up in a poaching expedition organized, as are most initiatives in the film, by Douggie, Pusey goes through an emotional and physical trauma which ends with his arrest for poaching and his discovery that the magistrate he will be coming up before is none other than the Laird he has (inadvertently) pushed into the Crinan Canal. The social research underlying *The Maggie* is faultless. The Laird is the only kilted figure in the film and speaks with an impeccable Home Counties accent, recalling Mackendrick's wish on *Whisky Galore!* (vetoed by Danischewsky) to put Waggett into a kilt. As Mackendrick would have known, with the Heritable Jurisdictions Act of 1746 in the wake of the failed Jacobite Uprising, the Scottish aristocracy and gentry lost their feudal obligations to their tenants and became more in the way of landlords. They were increasingly absorbed into the British upper class – while at the same time professing their Scottishness ever more – and began to adopt the mores of that class including sending their progeny to English public schools. Thus was created, in Scotland generally and in the Highlands and Islands in particular, a ruling class increasingly remote from those they ruled and speaking with the accents of outsiders. The Laird in *The Maggie* is archetypal of this class. It will be recalled that Gavin Wallace had posed the issue of whether Compton Mackenzie might have been critical of some aspects of Tartanry and Kailyard only to succumb to others. As will be seen, Mackendrick may have been caught in the same trap.

Marshall's destruction cannot be delayed indefinitely and is resumed when he himself boards the puffer to take charge of his cargo and arrange its transfer. The destruction is very carefully orchestrated, with incidents of rising intensity, and seems to have had several more stages at script level than appear in the film. There is, in the FSS, a 'missing' scene in which Mactaggart returns drunk to the puffer singing, 'I'm ower young to marry yet' and offers to teach Marshall some of 'the old airs'; in which Marshall cannot understand Douggie's Scots tongue; and in which his sleep is interrupted by Hamish's love-making. The scene ends with the following direction: 'MARSHALL's head appears for a few seconds above the level of the window. His expression is impossible to describe.'

In the film as we have it, the path to Marshall's destruction mounts with two dramatic reversals, one of them verbal, the other physical. Mactaggart, citing his 'seaman's intuition', forecasts a change in the weather, even fog. Marshall snorts 'Fog!' dismissively whereupon there is a cut to him peering through a pea-souper. In a later scene, with the puffer beached and waiting for the tide to lift it off, Marshall insists that Mactaggart accompany him on a ten-mile walk across the sand to reach a telephone, telling him, 'The exercise will do you good.' This is immediately followed (there is an intervening stage in the FSS) by Mactaggart strolling into their destination with Marshall hirpling in behind him. The film plays Marshall like a fish, hauling him in then letting him go temporarily. Such a letting go occurs after the two reversals described above. After he has been seduced by the breakfast Douggie has made (he confesses it is the heartiest meal he has eaten for months), the FSS describes him as follows: 'MARSHALL leans back and stretches powerfully. For the first time he is showing a certain relaxation of tension as if the long walk of the previous day, the night's deep sleep, the sea air and the big breakfast have combined to do him good.'

In this scene, there is a kind of wary communication emerging between Marshall and Douggie. However, this is simply the calm before the storm. In a series of escalating incidents (some of which, though in the FSS, do not appear in the film) there occurs the moment of Marshall's destruction. He has disembarked his cargo from the puffer and has it on the quayside waiting for a more orthodox vessel to pick it up, while

8. 'Like a penitent in a religious ceremony': the humiliation of
   Marshall.

'The Maggie' lies tethered to the ancient and rickety pier. Once again,
it is Douggie who points out the implications of the way the puffer is
tethered: when the tide comes in, 'Will there no' be an ... *accident?*'
Marshall's moment of greatest humiliation is in some respects reminiscent of Waggett's darkest moment as his wife's laughter rises on the
soundtrack. The derisive chorus here is provided by a group of Highland
cattle on the pier. Marshall, waiting on the pier with the tide rising,
begins to hear strange noises which may or may not be the lowing of
the cattle. Eventually he notices that the noises are coming from the pier
itself as, with the rising tide, the puffer, protruding under the pier,
begins to push it upwards. Marshall drags Mactaggart from the pub, the
latter affecting not to understand what Marshall is trying to tell him
about the puffer and the pier. Like the earlier scene in the Glasgow
hotel, events become 'bedlamized' by the involvement of the rest of the
puffer's crew and when Mactaggart belatedly 'understands' what Marshall is trying to tell him the tide is so high and the puffer lodged so
firmly under it that the pier starts coming apart. Marshall, by now totally
berserk, proceeds to stamp his feet on the splintering boards, eventually
going through them and ending up lying prostrate, like a penitent in a
religious ceremony. This, then, is the scene as realized in the film. The
FSS is much less cruel, simply having Marshall isolated on a broken

section of the pier and the incoming ship's captain chuckling over Mactaggart's guile. Just as with the fate of Waggett, the viewer is left wondering how a figure for whom Mackendrick professed sympathy (in an exchange of letters in *Time* magazine on the film's release in America) could be subjected to such cruel humiliation. Further evidence, later in the film and in the FSS, suggests that Mackendrick was ambivalent about Marshall, for he has not been broken and humiliated for nothing, nor is his penitential posture wholly accidental. When the dust from the incident has settled, the incoming captain asks if he is Mr Marshall. The reply is resonant: 'I'm no longer absolutely sure.'

It might be thought that nothing more can happen to Marshall, but Mackendrick adds one further cruel twist of the knife. Abased, and reluctantly having accepted that the puffer is the only boat that can take his cargo, he sets sail thinking that now, finally, he is on the last leg of his journey. He is puzzled first of all by the appearance on deck of a duck, then a child, then he is poleaxed to learn that, far from heading directly to his destination, Mactaggart has diverted to attend a birthday party at Bellabegwinnie for the centenarian Davy Macdougall. Marshall's look of consternation, as he is introduced to a succession of Macdougalls, turns to one of abject horror as the final member of the family, Miss Macdougall – a gargantuan woman seen only from the rear – erupts from the bowels of the ship like Mephistopheles from Hell.

Marshall has indeed been stripped of his identity as controlling tycoon – the trajectory of the film as a whole – but he has been broken in order to be remade, and the next scene gives a clue to his new identity. He changes, as the FSS describes it, into 'a heavy, turtle-necked sweater, dungarees and seaman's boots'. It is also no accident that it is in this scene that he has the last telephone call from his wife. She hangs up on him. He is now alone, totally cut off from his former life. It is at this point that *The Maggie* goes into ideological overdrive, both at the level of the FFS and the film as realized, and the Scottish Discursive Unconscious achieves its purest expression. We see now that Marshall has not undergone a simple change of clothes; he has been enrobed for entry into the mystical Other that, within the Scottish Discursive Unconscious, is the dream Scotland. Mackendrick's *mise-en-scène*, however, renders timeless and transcendental what, in the FSS, is only hinted at. In the FSS there is a fairly lavish party for the centenarian with some degree of ritual implied in the bringing of gifts to the old man who sits on a raised dais. Mackendrick heightens the sense of ritual and otherness by means of the music, the lighting and, although this is not entirely clear,

9. 'Marshall (Paul Douglas) is led into the dance by 'the Spirit of Scotland' (Fiona Clyne).

by making the old man blind. His age and (apparent) blindness associate him with the seers of Gaelic tradition such as are encountered in the writings of James 'Ossian' Macpherson. He speaks only Gaelic, so Marshall's words have to be interpreted to him by Mactaggart, thereby heightening the sense of otherness and ritual. Again, the film's social research is faultless. In 1951 there were still alive in the Highlands and Islands over two thousand Gaelic monoglots (including a kinswoman of my own). The playing and the pacing of the scene – Marshall is inducted slowly and reluctantly into the company – heightens the mood, as does the old man's not understanding Marshall's greeting to him that, where he comes from, they say the first hundred years are the hardest. When Mactaggart repeats the greeting in Gaelic, there is a long silent pause as the old man takes it in, and when he begins to laugh the music starts up and Marshall is given food and drink – whisky, of course. One more thing remains to complete the ideological project of this sequence. The differences between this final moment in the FSS and in the film are instructive. The FSS reads:

> [MARSHALL] turns to find that a ravishingly attractive GIRL of nineteen or twenty has approached him with a gay directness and is holding out her hands to him. MARSHALL tries to protest once more, but the ENGINEMAN gives him a little push. The GIRL takes his hands and pulls him out onto the floor. Once again MARSHALL tries to withdraw, but the delightful creature seems sure of herself and not to be denied. Very awkwardly at first he begins to dance ... The four from the Maggie shout encouragement.

In the FSS, Marshall's change is simply psychological. As realized in the film, however, it has become transcendental, indeed *ideological*. The puffer's crew do not figure in the film's version, as they do in the script. The girl advances, looking directly into the camera. Superficially reminiscent of a similar shot at the *réiteach* in *Whisky Galore!*, this shot has the feel of Marshall being inducted into the dream Scotland by the Spirit of Scotland. This moment represents the playing out of the Scottish Discursive Unconscious just as in *Brigadoon* and, later, *Local Hero*, in which, it will be recalled, the two Scots women are called Stella and Marina, the stars and the sea, Scotland as Nature. Thus is Compton Mackenzie's 'feminine' Scotland realized in *The Maggie* and the regressive discourses about gender and ethnicity intertwined. These will further interlace with the class discourse in the following scene which, more than any in Mackendrick's oeuvre, has elicited critical opprobrium. Philip Kemp's acount of this scene is worth quoting at some length. He describes it as

> the worst scene in the movie – perhaps the worst in any Mackendrick movie. Sitting out at the party with Sheena, the young woman who invited him to dance, Marshall is treated to a sententious parable about her two suitors: a handsome and ambitious trader and a fisherman ... [whom she chooses because] 'He'll not be so interested in what he's trying to do, or where he is going to ... And when we are very old we'll have only what we've been able to make together for ourselves – and I think perhaps that is all we'll need.' Cut to Marshall gloomily contemplating the error of his ways. Nowhere else in Mackendrick's work is the message thumped home so crudely ... We might take it for a last-minute insertion, a desperate attempt to wrench the film back on course, were it not that the whole scene, with scarcely a word changed, is right there in the shooting script [the FSS]. Such over-insistence betrays a

lack of conviction on the film-makers' part. Consciously or not, they had run themselves into an impasse. On the one hand, the values supposedly being celebrated – freedom, independence, the pride of tradition, the dignity of the individual – could find no credible correlative in the film as it stands. Only on the most sentimental and fuzzy level could the puffer crew ... be seen as a worthwhile embodiment of these qualities. On the other hand, the narrative line to which Mackendrick was committed didn't leave him space to do what he would ingeniously bring off in *The Ladykillers*, turn the whole thing into a subversive critique of just that kind of sentimental attitude. Comparison with *The Ladykillers*, or come to that, with *Whisky Galore!*, also reveals in *The Maggie* a failure to achieve the mythic quality that could lend the story resonance.[13]

Kemp is correct to point to the toe-curling sentimentality of this scene, but mistaken in the reasons he gives for it. It is precisely because the mythic elements triumph over the purposive, controlling elements that Mackendrick/Rose have so obviously lost control of the scene. To raise once more the distinction between conscious and unconscious elements in the shaping of a film, the conscious elements are the filmmakers' shaping of the script structure, the deployment of the *mise-en-scène* during shooting, and the process of editing; the unconscious elements are those deeply sedimented narratives, principally about class, gender and ethnicity, within which the filmmakers were born and raised, within which they were, to use Althusser's term again, *interpellated* and which they would regard as natural. In the writing and mounting of the previous dance scene and this one, the Scottish Discursive Unconscious – that dominant narrative about Scotland in which the land is magical and, above all, has the capacity to enchant and transform the stranger – comes bubbling to the surface and all but puts the FSS, but more strikingly the film, on to automatic pilot. But the filmmakers' loss of control is not as complete as Kemp avers. He suggests that Sheena's entire speech is followed by a 'cut to Marshall gloomily contemplating the error of his ways'. In fact, the cutting is more complex than that. Following Marshall's observation that the merchant is the obvious choice for her to marry since he can look after her and give her all the things she needs, she responds: 'It would be exciting to be married to a man who is going to do big things, who will go so far in the world ...' Here there is a cut from Sheena to Marshall on whose face the camera remains for the next few lines of Sheena's speech: '... It would be exciting to be taken to places, to be given fine clothes and expensive presents. Yes, I would like all those things ...'

Marshall's face is a study in misery as she utters these words, for he recognizes she is describing his own relationship with his wife who, it will be recalled, has severed contact with him just a couple of scenes earlier. The camera goes back to Sheena for her line, 'But I think it will be the other one I will be taking ... ' and back once more to Marshall for his surprised 'Why?' and his disintegrating face as Sheena continues:

SHEENA V/O: Oh, it's simply that even although he's away with his brothers so much, he'll have more time for me. He'll not be so interested in what he's trying to do, or where he's going to, because he'll just be fishing. And when he's come home from the fishing, there'll just be me. And when we're very old we'll have only what we've been able to make together for ourselves.

The camera goes back briefly to Sheena:

SHEENA: And I think perhaps that is all we'll need.

before closing on Marshall's embarrassed termination of the encounter. As the FSS puts it: 'But during this speech, despite the touching simplicity of SHEENA's thoughts, our attention is increasingly held by MARSHALL's reaction to them. He stares at her, his face set in an expression of terrible despair. With each artless phrase, SHEENA seems to deal him a bitterly savage blow.'

Incidentally, *pace* Mackendrick and Charles Barr (who is also unimpressed by what he describes as 'Douglas' graceless, one-note performance'), Douglas plays the scene rather sensitively, registering a quite diverse set of emotions – shame, regret, despair – as Sheena speaks. Clearly, then, the filmmakers are very much in control of the mechanics of this scene, playing out, as it were, Marshall's own relationship with his wife. Clearly, also, they are aware of the values they are counter-posing between Sheena and Marshall. What they are *not* aware of, however, is that, far from being 'artless' and of 'touching simplicity', Sheena's words are a classic restatement of the dominant narrative about Scotland and the Scots of the last two centuries. Sheena, in other words, is articulating the Scottish Discursive Unconscious. What Sheena is saying and the values she is espousing amount precisely to the role Malcolm Chapman describes history as having allocated the Celts:

the Ossianic controversy promoted a picture of the Celt as natural, emotional, naïve and a failure in the rough and tumble of the modern world. This Celt soon began to occupy a place in European history [and so were constructed] the qualities that were going to dominate future debate – sentimentality, impressionality, femininity and, perhaps the most quoted phrase in the history of Celtic Studies, a readiness to 'react against the despotism of fact'.[14]

The consciousness that the FSS reveals about Marshall's despair perhaps does not come across particularly clearly in the film. In this context, there is a scene in the FSS, immediately following the above scene with Sheena, in which Marshall, hopelessly drunk, has to be put to bed by the crew of the puffer. The FSS adds: 'It is a pathetic scene. There is nothing funny about it. If there is music here it is the saddest music we have ever heard.'

Although the three scenes of Marshall's destruction on the pier, his induction into the dream Scotland by way of the seaman's apparel and his involvement in the dance, and his exchange with Sheena, constitute the *ideological* high-water mark of the film, curiously they do not mark its dramatic crest. The *mise-en-scène* informs us that this occurs in a later scene. Even after Marshall's destruction and induction, the overall narrative structure of the shifting hegemony between Marshall and Mactaggart continues and appears to shift decisively to Marshall when he informs Mactaggart that he has bought the puffer out from under him by having Pusey contact Sarah in Glasgow, and that, having got a new crew to take his cargo to its destination, will sell the puffer for scrap. His announcement, and Mactaggart's response to it, are realized in the largest, most dramatic close-ups in the film, and with the most dramatic musical accompaniment. As is so throughout the film, it is Douggie who retrieves the situation by the drastic step of dropping a table top on Marshall's head. As it happens, Sarah refuses to sell, once more – and decisively this time – transferring the advantage back to Mactaggart. This again *appears* to slip away when the puffer runs on to the rocks and Mactaggart orders its abandonment, indicating to Marshall that, although the puffer is now doomed, he has twelve hours within which he can retrieve his cargo. It is at this point that the film once more takes off into ideological space. In order to save the puffer, Marshall orders his valuable cargo to be jettisoned. The same ideological manoeuvre is deployed at the end of *Rockets Galore!* when the proposed Hebridean rocket range is abandoned in favour of a bird sanctuary and at the end of *Local Hero* when the proposed oil terminal gives way to an observatory and a centre for marine conservation. It has been argued that a concept like the Scottish Discursive Unconscious is only partly about how Scotland and the Scots are represented in discourse; it is also about the relationship between that representation and the socio-political reality of Scotland and the extent to which the discourse may mask that reality and operate congenially on behalf of powerful forces. *Whisky Galore!* and *The Maggie* are widely read as beneficent and flattering to the Scots by showing how our 'innate' intelligence will thwart outsiders who seek to impose their values on our 'Edenic' land. Once more, we must recall from where this apparently beneficent discourse is spoken (and in whose interest): invariably metropolitan England and/or Hollywood. The fact that Mackendrick (arguably) and Bill Forsyth, writer/director of *Local Hero*, are Scots adds a truly chilling dimension: so hegemonic is the Scottish Discursive Unconscious, so absent are alternatives to it, that Scots themselves live within it! A glance at the history of modern (particularly Highland) Scotland will indicate the gulf between what Scots are imagined to do, the autonomy over their own country they are posited to wield, in films such as *Whisky Galore!*, *The Maggie* and *Local Hero*, and what actually happens in the 'real' world of politics and economics. The autonomy and prosperity of Scotland in relation to the UK as a whole is a con-tentious question, and by no means a static one. Marked changes occurred in the relationship with, for example, the setting-up of the welfare state in 1945 and in the more recent setting-up of the European Union and the Scottish Parliament. Careful analysis would therefore be required to assess whether, in purely material terms, Scotland benefits or loses from being part of the United Kingdom. The situation of the Highlands and Islands is rather more straightforward. Post-1745, and most markedly until 1945, it is a story of evictions, depopulation, absentee landlordism, economic stagnation and emigration. Writing in 1968, Ian Grimble described the situation of the Gael as follows:

> The Gael has in fact reached the end of the road along which he first began to retreat when Celtic Britain was first invaded by English-speak-ing settlers over a millennium and a half ago ... [T]he Gaels in Scotland have reached the peripheries of the Atlantic and remain there as a protected species, their affairs ordered for them by strangers with scarcely any reference to their wishes or requirements. The final step in this process was the creation of a Highland Development Board having as little connection with Highland society as the American Control Com-mission to Japan ... Unlike the Japanese, [the Gaels] were not defeated by a foreign power. They have simply been squeezed by degrees out of

a country they once owned, and their language reduced from one of the most literate in Europe to the status of a redundant peasant dialect.[15]

Reductive though this may be in certain respects, there is enough truth in it to confirm that Highland society stands absolutely no chance against central government, European banks owning large Highland estates, and international capitalism. The gulf between this fact and what *Whisky Galore!*, *The Maggie*, *Rockets Galore!* and *Local Hero* say about Highland Scotland is made possible by the hegemony of the Scottish Discursive Unconscious.

By having Marshall jettison his cargo to save the puffer, the makers of *The Maggie* probably thought they were simply endorsing a set of alternative, more humane, values against the corrupt individualism of capitalism. They were unaware that they were slotting into the Scottish Discursive Unconscious, that deeply sedimented narrative about Scotland which, over two centuries and more, beckons any who would write about, photograph or make any kind of image of Scotland. At a conscious level, however, they were still very much in control of the shape of the movie, further turning the knife into Marshall for dramatic effect. It is when the first massive crate is poised for jettisoning that Mactaggart (again under Douggie's prompting) reveals that he had not got round to insuring the cargo. Following the jettisoning, there is one last confrontation between Marshall and Mactaggart in which the latter hesitantly offers Marshall his money back and the latter seems ready to take it. In a final demonstration of Douggie's intelligence, he asks Marshall why he has bothered to save the puffer from the rocks only to remove the financial means to repair its plates and keep it in business. With a last gesture of resignation, Marshall thrusts the cheque back into Mactaggart's hand and departs to meet his wife who, we are told, is waiting at a local hotel. It seems that it was Mackendrick's original intention, until Rose wrote her off the screen, to have Marshall's wife return to him precisely because he has abandoned his capitalist values. This is not explicit in the film itself, although there is a hint of it; as Marshall strides away from the crew of the puffer, there is reprised the Gaelic song which had been played as background to Sheena's monologue about the superiority of Nature over Trade, suggesting that Marshall has been permanently affected by his encounter with the dream Scotland. This ending is perhaps too low-key and restrained for a popular cinematic comedy, so the actual ending is homologous with the opening of the film. The same two Glasgow harbour officials who, at the beginning, had signalled that Mactaggart

10.   *The individual versus the community. Marshall and the crew in*
      the final confrontation.

and the puffer were a source of trouble, sight the vessel again. One of
them asks the other whether he has ever heard of a puffer called the
'Calvin B. Marshall'. Thus is achieved the kind of resolution of contra-
diction to which popular cinema as a whole aspires, but lest the ending
be seen as *too* cosy, as we see the puffer steaming up the Clyde we hear
once more the unremitting argument between Mactaggart and the
Engineman with the latter's chainsaw voice telling him that he is 'not
even fit to be the skipper of the Govan ferry'.

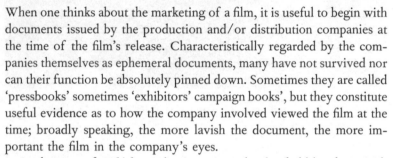

THREE
Post-production: Marketing and Consuming

When one thinks about the marketing of a film, it is useful to begin with documents issued by the production and/or distribution companies at the time of the film's release. Characteristically regarded by the companies themselves as ephemeral documents, many have not survived nor can their function be absolutely pinned down. Sometimes they are called 'pressbooks' sometimes 'exhibitors' campaign books', but they constitute useful evidence as to how the company involved viewed the film at the time; broadly speaking, the more lavish the document, the more important the film in the company's eyes.

In the case of *Whisky Galore!*, two pressbooks (held by the British Film Institute) are extant, one more lavish than the other. One is tempted to speculate – though there is no corroborating evidence – that the smaller one represents Ealing's initial low-key view of the film (it will be recalled that Balcon considered releasing it as a sixty-minute feature) and the latter Ealing's rethink following the film's unexpected success in the UK and elsewhere. The smaller of the two consists of four modestly-phrased pages: a synopsis, an introduction by Compton Mackenzie, and a brief essay (illustrated by photographs mainly of the shoot) by Monja Danischewsky. Mackenzie's piece is rather by way of placing his imprimatur on the film. Unlike his disparaging reference to the film in his memoirs, here he speaks very warmly of the experience: 'For the first time I have been able to enjoy the usually exasperating process of turning one of my books into a film.' It was not unusual at this time for film companies to stress the literary origins of their products. Indeed, if the adaptation was of a 'great book' they would often begin the film with an image of the book and proceed to turn the pages and dissolve into the film. Danischewsky's piece is partly a thank-you note to the residents of Barra, but is mainly an account of the unusual conditions of the shoot: 'Ealing Studios' first experiment in the Mobile Studio Unit'. There is no sense of this being a high-powered selling document. However, some of the facts Danischewsky reveals were to surface in subsequent reviews of the film.

The more lavish pressbook is clearly of a later vintage (it carries excerpts from the first round of reviews) and has the more aggressive tone of exhibitors' campaign books. Its first page carries the hucksterish slogan, 'Be prepared: Bookings galore for *Whisky Galore!*', and has brief synopses of the film in both French and Italian, publicity stills are offered, about a dozen publicity slogans are suggested (e.g. 'A Highland fling on a tight little island', 'The Highlands aren't dry lands any more' and 'Contraband is always risky, Yo ho ho, and a bottle of whisky!') and the longest section is headed 'Press Stories'. The latter contains little 'human interest' anecdotes, mostly about the cast, for instance that Joan Greenwood had problems getting her hair washed on Barra, and that Henry Mollison (Farquarson the exciseman) was reunited with five local men who had been interned with him in a German POW camp during the war. The overall tone, in common with the film, is very light, but the more lavish of the two pressbooks is very clearly a marketing tool. By this stage of *Whisky Galore!*'s life, Ealing clearly thought they had something worth selling.

Whisky Galore! was premièred in London on 16 June 1949 and in New York in December of that year and opened to almost universal acclaim among press reviewers. This was to continue in the United States and in continental Europe. The only sour note seems to have been the threat by temperance organizations in Denmark to boycott the film. The Danish response tells us as much about Danish culture as about the film itself. Although the Copenhagen reviewers were very warm, opposition seems to have been centred in rural Jutland. A temperance leader, a provincial newspaper editor, asked about his attitude to the film, replied: 'If drinking in the film is portrayed as pleasurable, I am very much in favour of a protest.'

More puzzlingly, the Danish censorship board gave it a certificate allowing it to be seen only by adults. Asked about their reasons, the chief censor replied: 'There is in this film an obvious disregard for ordinary legislation, in this case the law against smuggling, which is ridiculed through the circumvention of authority. Also, we believed that it was damaging for children to see alcohol portrayed as an absolute necessity for normal self-expression.'[1]

The chill hand of the ghost of temperance reached out in the United States as well, where, due to concerns expressed by the film industry's

11. *This montage from a German publicity leaflet not only shows a stunned Waggett (Basil Radford) bottom left, but also George Campbell (Gordon Jackson), bottom right after he has played his mother into silence and, top right, having his courage wound up by Doctor Maclaren (James Robertson Justice) so he can face her.*

self-censorship mechanism, the Production Code Administration, *Whisky Galore!* was retitled *Tight Little Island*. There is further evidence that, far from 'seeing' the same film, particular national audiences (and doubtless sub-groups within these audiences) 'remake' each film in terms of their own national narratives. Pierre Sorlin, exploring continental Europe's response to British films over half a century, writes about Italian responses to British films in general and Ealing comedies in particular:

> The 1950s were an epoch of violent political conflicts in most Continental countries, with liberal parties, especially the Christian Democrats, taking control from the communists and the left. Many cinema-goers were thus impressed by the description of firmly settled British communities and often missed the hints of much subtler divisions, such as the opposition between the English and the Scots in *Whisky Galore!*[2]

Sorlin's general point is interesting although, as Jeffrey Richards has argued, the Islanders' opposition is less to the English per se (after all, Sergeant Odd is an ally) than to a certain kind of bureaucratic book-soldiering. Incidentally, Sorlin adds that the Ealing comedies were much more generally popular in Italy than Italian distributors had expected, being among the few foreign films to play successfully in provincial cinemas.

In 1949 there were many more national and local papers than there now are, but it is the response of the nationals which is more readily accessible since the British Film Institute has maintained cuttings files on all new releases in the UK since the 1930s. Although more numerous in 1949, newspaper film reviewers then defined their role very much as they do nowadays – as consumer guides for their readers. What this means, then and now, for the most part, is a brief account of the story of the film and expressions of personal taste about (mainly) the performances but, in more serious papers, the writing, direction, cinematography and overall value of the film as entertainment might be commented upon. This 'consumer guide' element is evident in the kind of thumbnail summing-up of many of the reviews:

> ... rollicking fun with a Gaelic tang (*The Star*)
> ... gives you laughs galore (*Sunday Dispatch*)
> ... as pleasant a film as you could wish to see (*Sunday Graphic*)
> ... peppered with brilliant little cameos (*Sunday Pictorial*)
> ... will give you the pleasant warm glow that so eminently befits such a subject (*Evening Standard*).

The reviewer of the *Daily Telegraph*, while responding to the film's 'innocent pleasure', was almost alone in thinking 'that it would have been twice as funny at half the length'. The response in America was even more enthusiastic, with American reviewers discerning a particularly British flavour to the comedy:

There can be no doubt that [the film-makers] loved their work, and we have no doubt either that a lot of people over here are going to love this remarkable picture again and again. For *Tight Little Island* is another happy demonstration of that peculiar knack British movie-makers have for striking a rich comic vein in the most unexpected and seemingly insular situations. (*Variety*)

With regard to the response of British reviewers, certainly at that time – it is an open question if things are different today – film reviewing had a very low status in newspapers. No special awareness of (or even interest in) cinema was thought necessary to become a film reviewer. As a consequence, much of the reviewing has a 'hack' or dilettante quality to it. This contrasts markedly with the razor-sharp precision of the reviews in the film trade press which were written *by* film people *for* film exhibitors who wanted to know exactly what a particular film would deliver for their patrons. The review of *Whisky Galore!* in *Today's Cinema* is exemplary in this respect:

Clever direction and interesting treatment lend enchantment to a simple story skilfully told, brilliantly characterised and presented against magnificent natural backgrounds. Sly comedy, robust humour, sly romance and forthright dialogue provide apt comment on island life and manners. Wholly convincing atmosphere; neat development; hilarious climax; grim wreck and salvage incidents. Superbly natural portrayals by carefully selected cast, among whom it would be invidious to make distinctions. First class production values include clear recording of fascinating dialect. Refreshing and appealing entertainment for any and every audience and with obvious box-office angles.

There are several intriguing features about the British film reviewers' responses to *Whisky Galore!* There is, for example, the dawning realization that something special in the way of comedy is beginning to emerge from Ealing:

The fact that it was made by the same studio as *Passport to Pimlico* suggests that Sir Michael Balcon has a corner in adult humour. (*Sunday Express*)

Once more, from Ealing Studios, the stronghold of British film humour, comes a picture to chase the blues away. (*Evening News*)

Apparently the British studios are at last learning something about comedy – or at least one British studio is. (*Daily Worker*)

Ealing Studios are making a gallant effort to prove that the British can produce good comedies. Their success to date is largely the result of their choice of uniquely British subjects treated in a wry, gentle, good-humoured way (*Evening Standard*).

This last quotation goes some way to the consensual definition of an 'Ealing comedy' that would be firmly in place within half a decade.

As John Ellis has pointed out in 'The Quality Film Adventure: British Critics and the Cinema 1942–1948', one of the tenets of the call for a 'quality cinema' at this time was that the fusion of documentary and fiction should be central. The idea of 'realism' has seldom been far from the British critical sensibility – 1930s documentary and its transposition into wartime feature film production and the so-called 'British New Wave' of the 1960s were other such moments. There was, therefore, a strong impulse in many of the reviews to celebrate those aspects of *Whisky Galore!* which might be constructed as 'realist':

> ... a picture which exploits racy humour, homely characters, wild beauty of the scenery with the detailed realism of a documentary feature. (*The Star*)

> ... the aesthetic island backgrounds including both seascapes and the only island bar; and the local extras, give the film a delicious and authentic flavour. (*Reynolds News*)

> ... a great deal of the freshness of the piece ... is due to the fact that there was no hiatus between indoor and outdoor shooting: the indoor passages as well as the scenes on the shore and in the moonlit harbour streets were photographed on the Isle of Barra. (*Sunday Times*)

> *Whisky Galore!* was made entirely on location in the Isle of Barra in the Hebrides and it is doubtful whether any finer example of truthful recording could be found among film archives. The film achieves a simple realism and conviction that could not have been secured in a studio with the same effect of artless charm. (*Today's Cinema*)

This dimension of the reviewers' response, the fact that it was so widespread and the fact that Mackendrick too had documentary cinema in mind in his parodic introduction to the film suggest that there may be certain prominent art discourses at play in a society at a particular time within which artworks are not only coded but decoded, almost irrespective of the other dimensions of the artworks.

As was argued previously, both *Whisky Galore!* and *The Maggie* were constructed within certain unconscious discourses, the most important of which relate to class, gender and ethnicity. With regard to the unconscious ethnic discourse, precisely because these reviews were very largely written by metropolitan, middle-class Englishmen (and, to a very much lesser extent, women), they inhabit the same mind set, *vis-à-vis* Scotland and the Scots, as did the makers of *Whisky Galore!* That is, they too were shaped within the Scottish Discursive Unconscious. As a consequence, a symptomatic reading can be made of the reviews which will demonstrate what the writers felt to be the commonsense, 'natural' view of Scotland and the Scots. Again, we should recall Malcolm Chapman's remarks about the range of terms within which the Celt has been historically constructed:

> [Mackendrick] has a deft touch, a subtle appreciation of character, and an informed mind on the ways of those whose riches are not measured by commercial standards. (*Today's Cinema*)
>
> This is a comedy of the Outer Hebrides – and as gentle and beguiling as the voices of the islanders. (*Daily Graphic*)
>
> ... its savour of open seas, island mountains and gentle folk who are only the more amusing because of their basic simplicity and natural cunning. (*Evening News*)
>
> ... the story is freaked with the sort of fancy that is half childlike and half agelessly wise. (*Sunday Chronicle*)

It is not simply the British reviewers who live within the Scottish Discursive Unconscious. Its international hegemony is illustrated by the American response as well:

> Filmed entirely in the Hebrides where the faces are as roughhewn as the landscapes. (*Time*)

Surely, it might be thought, the reviewers of the Scottish press would have been more alert to the workings of the Scottish Discursive Unconscious, but – as has been suggested – so hegemonic is the dominant narrative about Scotland that even Scots themselves live within it. That said, there are certain differences between the Scots' coverage and that of other societies. There had long been a smouldering resentment against what was seen as metropolitan English condescension towards Scotland and this sometimes manifested itself in a tendency to feel insulted by 'external' image-making of the country. *Whisky Galore!* produced none of this usual resentment, although the review in the *Glasgow Herald* is seething with a readiness to be insulted and with hostility to the English. The tendency is obliquely referred to in the heading of the review '*Whisky Galore!* No Parody of the Scots' and the review begins:

> It is no concern of ours if English audiences enjoy *Whisky Galore!* for the wrong reasons and flatter themselves with the delusion that Basil Radford, an excellent performer, is the star. We in Scotland can convince ourselves that we are enjoying a private joke – a national and subtle one that cannot be fully savoured south of the border ... The effect is not that which we have had so often and so irritatingly before of a stranger setting a film in the Highlands and including local colour collected by a research team. It is rather of a native making a comedy and almost unconsciously drawing on his own experience and background.

Not for the last time, as will be demonstrated, the reviewer, in using the phrase 'unconsciously drawing on his own experience and background', says more than he was altogether aware of. The response of Scottish reviewers was generally warm although the occasional review might take an odd turn. It will be recalled that many of the London reviews were marked by a disposition to measure the film against 'reality', a by-product of the status of documentary realism, from the 1930s, through the wartime period, in British film culture. As it happened, Forsyth Hardy, acolyte to the high priest of the documentary movement, John Grierson, was film reviewer of *The Scotsman* at this time and, predictably, his review passes through the prism of the values he shared so ardently with Grierson:

> For a long time now writers on the cinema have been urging British film-makers to be out and about, to leave the walls of their studios behind and to take their cameras into the towns and villages, the hills and valleys of Scotland, England and Wales. Sir Michael Balcon ... whose work has always had the quality of real life to it, has allowed a group to do just that ... The result is that the vigorous, distinctive sense of place and character conveyed by Mr Compton Mackenzie in his novel has been carried over into the translation into the new medium.

With *The Maggie*, it is again useful to begin with the surviving promotional material since this indicates how Ealing Studios were thinking about the film in 1953. A fairly lavish pressbook survives in the British Film Institute collection, suggesting that Ealing were putting more resources into promotion than was the case at the time of *Whisky Galore!* It is extremely well illustrated with stills from the film which often capture key moments of the narrative; there are pictures of all the major players with biographies of each; and an extensive account of the shoot. All of this echoes the characteristics of the *Whisky Galore!* promotional material, but on a more lavish scale. The pressbook on *The Maggie* contains an additional feature which reflects a wider strategy of the British film industry in the 1950s. The Holy Grail of British film producers – as far back as Alexander Korda in the 1930s – had been to penetrate the American market. This was an ongoing concern in the post-war period, a particular strategy of the 1950s being to give individual films 'marquee value' in the United States by importing an American star (and sometimes director). Such had been the case with *Night and the City*, which had imported actor Richard Widmark and director Jules Dassin (although the latter's presence may have had more to do with his McCarthyite blacklisting in the United States). It might perhaps be more accurate to say that this 1950s strategy reprised that of the inter-war period during which Balcon himself, when he was head of production at Gaumont-British, presided over the policy of importing less than top-drawer American 'stars'. This appeared to be continuing with the casting of Robert Taylor in *A Yank at Oxford* when Balcon was, all too briefly, head of production of the British arm of Metro Goldwyn Mayer. In the case of *The Maggie*, the American star was Paul Douglas and the fact that he was American was much more integral to the story than was the case in other such importations. The centrality of Paul Douglas to the promotion of the film is reflected in his being the only name, apart from Balcon's, above the title, and in the separate feature on him in the pressbook. As will be seen, the film generated some debate about where its sympathies lay, specifically whether it presented the Paul Douglas character as duped or redeemed. The pressbook is in no two minds about this: 'Marshall loses all along the line. From it all, he begins to gain a new outlook on life, and appreciation of the more leisurely way of life instead of the ruthlessness of business activity ... And when the climax is reached ... he takes the decision which shows that Calvin B. Marshall has become humanized at last.'

As has been indicated, the major resource for researching film history in Britain is the British Film Institute and all the references thus far have been to material held in its collection. However, another source of historic material is the burgeoning commercial market in film-related 'ephemera' such as posters, stills and pressbooks. It was on this circuit that I picked up an 'Exhibitor's Campaign Book' on *The Maggie*. It is undated, but was produced by General Film Distributors, a distribution mechanism within which J. Arthur Rank had been prominent since its founding in 1935 and which, in the mid-1950s, did indeed mutate into J. Arthur Rank Film distributors and ultimately RFD. Unlike the press-book, the campaign book carries a lot of technical information about the various sizes of blocks available for press ads, about poster sizes, about stills, slides and trailers available and the financial terms for hiring them. GFD even had a scheme to share the costs of additional advertising with the theatres. Like the pressbook, however, the campaign book carries copies of slides and a similar series of 'human interest' stories about (mainly) the cast which might be placed in local media. More commercially aggressive than the pressbook, the campaign book has a list of suggestions to drum up local interest in the film, from inviting local girls called Maggie to the opening night to decorating local shop windows 'to symbolise the progress and love of tradition in industry. Compare modern cotton frocks with an old spinning wheel; fluorescent lamps with an old oil lamp; a modern radiogram with an old crystal set.' Several advertising slogans are suggested, including one which indicates the tradition the distributors felt the film to be in: 'You hooted at *Genevieve* ... now rock with *The Maggie*.' This was indeed the line that was taken up by the *News Chronicle* in its heading 'Sister for *Genevieve*'.

The Maggie opened in London on 25 February 1954 and in New York (under the title *High and Dry*) in September of that year. Press response was very much less uniformly welcoming than in the case of *Whisky Galore!* Although it had its out-and-out defenders –

The best British comedy for many a day! (*Daily Worker*)

Hurray for another sparkling Ealing comedy! ... This is a thoroughly entertaining film, the characters drawn with masterly precision, the situations original, the humour gentle. (*The Spectator*)

An enchanting Ealing film for anyone with both a heart and a sense of humour. (*Sunday Express*)

– many reviewers were of split mind or simply lukewarm in their response. Of Mackendrick and Rose, the reviewer of the *Sunday Times* wrote: 'I don't think either of this imaginative pair has fully worked out

his ideas to the end: at any rate the weakness of the film is in the last
quarter where the story, instead of gathering itself together loses its
compactness, speed. Still, I find it a delightful entertainment.' And the
reviewer of the *Daily Sketch*: 'Alas for the film, the tussle is too one-
sided. The Maggie's crew ... are delightful. But the unfortunate Douglas
is given no chance to develop into a character.'

Some reviewers compared *The Maggie* adversely with *Whisky Galore!*:

Alexander Mackendrick, who made *Whisky Galore!*, also made *The
Maggie*. It is unlikely that for this most recent essay in Highland whimsy
he will be as well remembered as for his previous adventure in the same
territory. *The Maggie* indeed is not a great film and in all objectivity it
could not even be described as a very good one. (*Manchester Guardian*)

... the captain, a whiskery old Scottish fraud, and his crew are obviously
supposed to have the same ne'er-do-well charm as the islanders of
Whisky Galore!: but somehow the note is all wrong. (*Sunday Chronicle*)

... it is all very cosy and consoling in the manner of *Genevieve* and
Whisky Galore! ... but it is less well sprung than those two winners and
is not shy of punching you in the ribs in case you miss the joke. (*Observer*)

It would seem that what is described herein as the richness and
complexity of the film's *mise-en-scène* was a source of confusion and
irritation to at least one reviewer of the time: 'The chief fault is technical.
There are too many crowded scenes and far too many background
noises.' (*Evening Standard*)

It would also seem that even the dilettante reviewers of the British
press were undergoing a change in 1954. There is nowhere near the
same comprehensive resort to 'realism' as a criterion of value such as
prevailed at the time of *Whisky Galore!*'s release, although it still makes
an occasional appearance:

The clear-washed landscapes of canal and waterway restfully hold the
eye. (*Financial Times*)

The picture was made entirely among the Western Islands. The scenery
– rocky coasts and slapping seas – is fine. (*Evening News*)

A feature of the film is the beauty of Scotland's own scenery, the Crinan
Canal area and the odd shots of land and coastline of the Inner Hebrides.
(*Dundee Courier and Advertiser*)

For many reviewers, Ealing Studios is now recognized as, par excellence, the hub of British cinematic comedy and the reviewer in *The Times* begins the review with a thumbnail sketch of what had, by then, become the popular view of Ealing (it would take Charles Barr's book twenty-three years hence to introduce a range of nuances into discussion of Ealing's output):

> All good sentimentalists – perhaps romantics would be the better word – must cherish a warm feeling for the products of the Ealing Studios. They are, these studios, so sturdily on the side of the small, the humble, the out-dated, the obstinately individualistic. They fight for the waywardness of things in a mechanical and efficient universe: they plead for the survival of all that is doomed by material progress not to survive.

Although, as with *Whisky Galore!*, the Scottish Discursive Unconscious lurks below several of the reviews – 'The dialect is Scottish, the wisdom the kind that enables Highlandmen to outwit any opposition they may encounter from across the border' (*Daily Mail*) – in the case of *The Maggie* the reviewers' sense of the otherness of Scotland generates a particularly pernicious sub-discourse which often comes into play when non-Scots are confronted by artefacts relating to Scotland – the adopting of a mock-Scottish mode of speaking or writing. The *Sunday Graphic* described Fiona Clyne – Sheena, the Spirit of Scotland woman who inducts Marshall into the Celtic world – as 'a cool and charming lassie with a beguiling burr' and the *Evening News* described Tommy Kearins (Douggie) as 'a bonny bairn'. But far and away the worst example is the *Daily Telegraph*'s '*The Maggie* ... is sae fu' o' bricht Scots dialect that I could have done wi' a wee subtitle, or even twa.' This kind of metropolitan condescension is sometimes practised by American reviewers. *Time* partakes of it in describing Tommy Kearins as 'a bonny little fiend' but is nowhere near as insulting as the *Daily Telegraph*. It does, however, 'caledonianize' the review by referring to stereotypical elements of Scotland. The film as a whole is called 'as salty as a whelk in the Firth of Forth', the puffer is described as looking like 'nothing so much as a seagoing haggis' and Alex Mackenzie is compared with Sir Harry Lauder. Nevertheless, it was *Time*'s very favourable review which was to provoke the most arresting comment on *The Maggie* in the form of a letter to the magazine (27 September 1954) from an American:

Sir:

One can cheer for the import of Scotch whisky but perhaps there ought to be a stiffer tariff on Scotch whimsy. The latest cinematic highball,

High and Dry [*The Maggie*'s American title] ... is every bit as charming as your excellent movie reviewer says it is, in fact so relentlessly charming that about halfway through one longs for a refreshing draught of Mickey Spillane. But underneath all the charm the picture is a perfect allegory of America's fate in Europe ... And so we come to the shot of the sinking crates containing (note symbolism) bathtubs and iceboxes. That's America in Europe: taken for our money, cheated, fooled, our advice ignored, our skills wasted, our intentions sneered at – and in the end we wind up thinking that it's our fault and that there is something morally and aesthetically fine about old rustbuckets ...

Fletcher Grimm

Grimm's letter produced a somewhat disingenuous reply from Mackendrick in the 25 October issue:

Reader Grimm is entirely right. I have been a little surprised that nobody else noticed the implications in the script of *High and Dry*. The satire was not buried very deep. It would be sad, however, if he thought there was malicious intent. Does it help to point out that Bill Rose ... is, like myself, an American. We saw the story very much from the viewpoint of the American. The savagely unfair way in which the American is treated, the sly insult added to injury and the penultimate indignity of being expected to feel that he is somehow 'morally' in the wrong were, for us, part of the flavour of the joke. Some British critics also complained about the way Mr Marshall was intolerably treated ... It just shows how dangerous it is to try to be funny in the field of international relationships.

Grimm's letter is all the more arresting for doing what practically no one, film reviewers included, did in the 1950s – taking popular cinema seriously. Although he speaks of it misleadingly as an 'allegory', Grimm is essentially saying that *High and Dry* constitutes anti-American Cold War propaganda. This may help explain the apparent disingenuousness of Mackendrick's reply. Few American filmmakers at this time (Mackendrick, it should be remembered, remained an American citizen and was probably aware that his stint at Ealing would come to an end) would have wished to put themselves in line for blacklisting by having one of their films read as anti-American. That said, Mackendrick is at one level correct. The FSS – less clearly the film – is suffused with sympathy for Marshall. Here, I would raise once more the distinction between the conscious and unconscious elements in *The Maggie*. At the conscious level, Mackendrick was clearly thinking in *moral* terms about the fate of Marshall. It was the unconscious ideological level which was floating free, as it were, travelling under automatic pilot, waiting to be read by those alert to ideological issues: Fletcher Grimm from a rather hawkish, patriotic American point of view, the present writer from the point of view of a Scot much preoccupied with how his native land and fellow-countrymen have been represented over several centuries. In a sense, Grimm's insight was two decades too early. Had his point been made in the 1970s, the theoretical and critical climate of the time would have been much more congenial to the kind of argument he was making and others may have picked up and run with the ball he set in motion. His letter remains as a fascinating exception to the dominant reviewing response to *The Maggie* which was broadly concerned to address it in terms of how it worked as a piece of entertainment.

The reviews which appeared in the Scottish press function within the same kind of critical discourse as the reviews elsewhere: the film is a piece of entertainment to be awarded marks in terms of the achievements of its individual personnel. However, the Scots reviewers, accustomed to confronting representations of their country and people fashioned elsewhere, had developed – as was seen in relation to *Whisky Galore!* – *some* sense of films as offering images of the place. Thus:

> Here indeed is a fine picture capturing the spirit of the West of Scotland and showing the world that men north of the border don't run around in kilts waving claymores all the time. (*Glasgow Evening News*)

> What England thinks of this picture is no concern of mine here. But I will tip it as a winner in Scotland … We are not depicted as so often we are depicted, as dour and dopey. (*Glasgow Evening Citizen*)

> *The Maggie* differs from most of the other Scottish films in that it was written direct for the screen. It is important that … there should be some films which spring direct from the life of the country. Otherwise the camera is deprived of its function as an observer and recorder. (*Weekly Scotsman*).

It will come as no surprise that the last of these quotations was written by Forsyth Hardy, hence the continuing recourse to Griersonian categories of value. However, all the Scottish reviews were agreed: *The Maggie* offers a sympathetic portrayal of the Scots. Indeed, the *Glasgow Evening News* serialized ecstatically in a dozen parts the novelization of the film. The warm response of the Scots reviewers is another chilling example (see Mackendrick himself and Bill Forsyth) of the extent to which the Scots themselves live within the Scottish Discursive Unconscious.

As has been mentioned, serious, academic critical writing about *Whisky Galore!* and *The Maggie* does not emerge until the appearance of Charles Barr's book on Ealing Studios in 1977, but there is a 1950s review of *The Maggie* which might be regarded as transitional between the popular and the academic: Karel Reisz's review in *Sight and Sound*. At one level, it reprises the worry expressed by the newspaper reviewers about the final quarter of the film – 'Only towards the end does the story run out of predicaments and switch to a not altogether successful passage of pathos' – but displays a sharper sense of performance and direction and their relationship:

> The direction is, for the most part, pleasantly discursive, yet retains a quick and flexible pace. Alex Mackenzie plays Mactaggart with unobtrusive skill and Mackendrick has obtained a beautifully tough and sensitive performance from Tommy Kearins. One among a number of good minor performances is immediately striking: Fiona Clyne plays her single, rather awkwardly written scene, with sincerity and just the right suggestion of latent temperament.[3]

This is the putative movie professional – Reisz was to go on to direct movies such as *Saturday Night and Sunday Morning*, *Morgan: a Suitable Case for Treatment*, *The Gambler* and *Dog Soldiers* – assessing the writing, playing and direction of the film with a sharper eye than the reviewers of the press, but when it comes to the representation of the Scots – whom he describes as 'simple fisher folk' – Reisz too is in thrall to the Scottish Discursive Unconscious: 'The director's observation of the islanders, affectionate, ironic and quite free from patronage, brings them to life with a fresh and sometimes touching humour. They are never allowed to go out of character for the sake of a joke, as they sometimes did in *Whisky Galore!*'[4]

Reisz and, on his say-so, Mackendrick, are constructing the Scots in terms not dissimilar to the way nineteenth-century ethnologists constructed the 'primitive' peoples of the world beyond Europe and on Europe's own peripheries. That is, serious and even academic writing on *The Maggie* (and *Whisky Galore!*) is quite as likely to be shaped by the dominant, unconscious narrative of Scotland. This is even true, however vestigially, of Charles Barr's analysis of *Whisky Galore!* in which he describes the Islanders as 'a community in whose capacity for survival we can believe. It embodies an ancestral Celtic shrewdness and toughness, from which we should learn.'[5]

In certain respects the project of Barr's book is not dissimilar to that of this volume. At one level, he is concerned to outline the essential *Englishness* of Ealing's films (a central project of Barr's writing as a whole), but within that he wishes to point to the diversity of Ealing's output and the fact that there were resistant as well as compliant sensibilities at play, the resistant sensibilities rightly being seen as of greater interest and complexity. There was a certain mode of British critical writing of the 1960s, particularly discernible among those critics who, like Barr, had some connection with the journal *Movie*. Doubtless produced by *Movie*'s polemical stance – broadly the rescuing from critical indifference of interesting auteurs – this form of critical writing set up a whipping-boy against whom the favoured auteur would be measured. In the context of Ealing comedy, Barr's whipping boy is T. E. B. Clarke, the compliant sensibility against whom are measured Robert Hamer and Alexander Mackendrick, the resistant sensibilities. As Barr puts it, the films of Hamer and Mackendrick are 'strong where the others are weak, tough where they are gentle, intelligent where they are at best ingenious'.[6]

It is precisely this toughness and intelligence that Barr goes on to argue for in his separate chapter on *Whisky Galore!*, on occasion getting into the detail of *mise-en-scène* as in the early scene in the Post Office involving Macroon, Waggett and Sergeant Odd, about which he writes: 'Given its importance, it is very striking that Mackendrick should present the whole post-office scene in the neutral manner he does and refrain from "signposting" what is going on – Waggett's obtuseness, Macroon's calculation, the temptation offered to the Sergeant – by any strong comic/dramatic emphasis in the cutting or playing.'[7]

Barr is here discerning the same fondness for the long take, and a revulsion for shot/counter-shot cutting, that has been demonstrated with regard particularly to the early scenes of *The Maggie*. Barr writes about the latter film not in a separate chapter but in one entitled 'Late Comedies'. One wonders if Barr is to some extent being driven by the logic of his critical project – the rise, until about 1951, of Ealing and its subsequent decline – rather than by the realization on screen of *The Maggie* itself. In a curious way, his response parallels that of the newspaper reviewers at the time of the film's release. Once more using Clarke as the touchstone to elevate Mackendrick, he goes on:

The Maggie has far more life and intelligence and moral tension than its Clarke equivalents. At the same time, it is no masterpiece. One sometimes senses an impatience in Rose and Mackendrick at what they are doing, as if they are trapped in a backwater, and with a *fiddling* set of conflicts and frustrations. This is the least satisfying of Mackendrick's quintet of Ealing films.[8]

Tony Williams, in *Structures of Desire: British Cinema, 1939–1955*, does not engage with Barr's assessment of *The Maggie*, but is critical of his warm response to *Whisky Galore!* Williams is preoccupied with the 'poverty of desire' of British cinema in general (and perhaps that of Ealing Studios in particular) and sees the Islanders' victory not as a triumph of freedom over constraint (the dominant view of the film), but as the imposition of an alternatively repressive system. Williams is provocative on the relationship between (primarily) sexual repression and socio-political repression, but his account of British cinema is innocent of any distinctions between the representation of the English and the Scots.

Barr's account of characters such as Mactaggart, Marshall and Douggie is almost wholly psychological (rather the way, perhaps, that Rose and Mackendrick thought of them), seeing Mactaggart as 'clever, but in a rather sterile way', Douggie as 'young, alert, less set in his ways than the others' and Marshall as far from being 'a blameless victim'. What is missing from Barr's account – unsurprisingly given the ethnic position from which he speaks – is any awareness of the *ideological* stakes at issue in *The Maggie*. For instance, the scene of the centenarian's party and the dance – described herein as the ideological high-water-mark of the film – is passed over by Barr as '[W]hen Marshall is moved by hospitality at a party, he makes a real concession'. The difference between Barr and the present writer in ascertaining what is of greatest importance in *The Maggie* poses the question once more of whether the text itself or the diverse identities of its readers is more important.

Philip Kemp's critical project is more singlemindedly auteurist than Barr's: 'The contention underlying this book is that all Mackendrick's work exhibits strong thematic and stylistic links ... Nor do the later films show signs of a falling off in Mackendrick's powers ... Their faults ... stem not from any lack of directorial skill, but from the circumstances under which they were produced.'[9]

The extent to which the present volume has resorted to quotation from Kemp's book indicates its centrality in discussions of Mackendrick's work. Its information-assembling, its range of references, its original research (it incorporates material from two extensive interviews Kemp did with Mackendrick) and its careful critical assessment of each of Mackendrick's films make it *the* authority on its subject. One's reservations have to do primarily with its critical method – auteurism's tendency to homogenize the auteur's films, to perceive connections among and impute coherence to all of its subject's films. This is most notable in the level of generality *thematic* auteurism is obliged to resort to in its linking of one film to another. Earlier, I described *Whisky Galore!* as having, by the nature of its staggered production process, a Frankenstein monster quality which makes it difficult to assign responsibility and which certainly, in my view, makes it difficult to describe it unambiguously as 'a Mackendrick film'. Kemp takes a different view:

> Mackendrick's first feature film introduces several elements characteristic of his work; it is, quite recognisably – to use the slightly suspect, shorthand term – 'a Mackendrick film.' Most evident is the theme which, first mooted in *Saraband* [*for Dead Lovers*, for which Mackendrick co-wrote the screenplay and designed the storyboards] is explored and reinterpreted in various aspects throughout his work: the confrontation between Innocence and Experience, here represented by Waggett on the one hand and the islanders on the other.[10]

The problem with this kind of auteurist analysis is whether it is specific enough to separate the work of its subject from that of many other film directors. What strong dramatic conflicts in cinema could not, at some level, be described as a clash between Innocence and Experience: Mr Deeds and the shyster lawyers in *Mr Deeds Goes to Town*; Joan of Arc and the Inquisition in *The Passion of Joan of Arc*; Kaspar Hauser and German society in *The Enigma of Kaspar Hauser*, and so on? Auteurists are on firmer ground when they attempt to demonstrate recurrences in their subjects' *mise-en-scène*. Kemp argues that: 'because Mackendrick is intent on allowing his audience to read a situation and compare what we see with what the characters within it are seeing, he rarely invites us to identify with the viewpoint of any single protagonist. Point of view shots are scarce in his films ... Generally his directorial perspective remains detached, ironically critical.'[11]

This is very close to what is being argued by Charles Barr with regard to the post office scene in *Whisky Galore!* and, indeed, what is argued in these pages with regard to the highly populated frame of that film and, more particularly, to the action in depth of field in *The Maggie*.

I am not aware if André Bazin – the great French proponent of (among other things) the long take that leaves the photographed world intact for us to make our own judgements about what is important in it – was familiar with Mackendrick's films, but he would certainly have approved of their *mise-en-scène*.

Kemp ventures into the terrain of the political implications of *Whisky Galore!* with two suggestions. One is that the film offers 'the highly subversive doctrine that the structure of authority can be rendered powerless by consensual action of the whole community – social anarchism in its essential form'.[12] Fair enough, but entrenched power in the real world has very little to fear from populist utopianism, heart-warming though it may appear when one is sitting in a cinema, with hundreds of others, all rooting for the underdog. Kemp's other political point about *Whisky Galore!* is that it 'could well be read as a satire on colonialism, with Waggett a mislocated Sanders of the River, exhorting the recalcitrant natives and making patronising little forays into what he sees as the quaint local lingo'.[13]

Just like films, critical texts can be read for their silences and it is here, in Kemp's text, that a yawning fissure opens up that the text itself is unaware of. In other words, Kemp, by throwing up the colonial metaphor, is saying more than he is conscious of. Unlike Barr, he does not articulate the Scottish Discursive Unconscious explicitly but, like Barr, he is innocent of its workings; again, not surprisingly, given the ethnic standpoint from which he speaks.

Opening his chapter on *The Maggie*, Kemp refers to Charles Barr's remarks about the later Ealing films' attachment to 'items that are … little and old' and Mackendrick's two late Ealing films *The Maggie* and *The Ladykillers* as at first sight conforming to this pattern. However:

> in both films the victory of the traditional forces is equivocal … Macken-drick's attitude to his decrepit symbols is fiercely ironic and the films are shot through with internal tensions which lend them a vitality rare in late-period Ealing. In *The Ladykillers* these tensions are contained within a framework of highly stylised black comedy. In the case of *The Maggie* the tensions are neither contained nor resolved and the film comes apart at the seams. *The Maggie* is generally rated the least satisfactory of Mackendrick's Ealing films.[14]

This seems an extraordinarily harsh judgement on *The Maggie* and is, indeed, qualified elsewhere in Kemp's chapter on it. Nevertheless, it would seem that both Barr and Kemp (and very likely Rose and Mackendrick) are 'blind' to a level of energy that is crackling throughout the film and which I have tried to describe in taking issue with Kemp's and Barr's reading of the linked scenes of Marshall's destruction and remaking within 'dream Scotland'. Clearly, the Scottish Discursive Unconscious is not something I approve of, but I find its delirious realization in these scenes so breathtaking that these moments (plus, of course, Mackendrick's sophisticated *mise-en-scène* throughout the film) confer on *The Maggie* a level of interest far in excess of that generated by *Whisky Galore!* For me, *The Maggie* does not 'come apart at the seams'. At the level of Mackendrick's *mise-en-scène* it is extremely controlled and at the level of the major unconscious ideology informing it – the Scottish Discursive Unconscious – it is all too coherent!

In the course of his discussion of *The Maggie*, Philip Kemp – in common with the more recent critics mentioned in the Introduction – engages with my own 1982 essay 'Scotland and Cinema: the Iniquity of the Fathers' which, in its synoptic scope, inevitably did not do justice to the complexity of *Whisky Galore!* and *The Maggie* and may, in certain details, have misdescribed them. To this extent, Kemp's strictures constitute fair comment. As mentioned previously, the thrust of *Scotch Reels* (the book in which my essay appeared) was polemical and ideological – to raise questions about the way Scotland and the Scots had been represented in film and television. It was wide-ranging and, with few exceptions, left no space for the kind of nuanced judgements such as are made by Barr and Kemp and, hopefully, the present volume. This being so, it was widely (mis)read as an outright, unqualified attack on the films it mentioned. I hope the foregoing analyses of *Whisky Galore!* and *The Maggie* will demonstrate what has always been the position of the contributors to *Scotch Reels*, that it is possible to deplore the ideologies within which certain films are constructed and yet to find them pleasurable and/or of absorbing interest.

Taken as a whole, both press and academic criticism of *Whisky Galore!* and *The Maggie* show the same bias which unambiguously favours the former. This is borne out by more objective indicators. Barely mentioning *The Maggie* in his memoirs – he refers to it in passing in the context of William Rose's work for Ealing within which *The Ladykillers* is given pride of place – Michael Balcon makes several warm references to *Whisky Galore!*, including the extent to which it was taken up by the Scotch whisky industry after it had become an international success. The Scottish Film Council ran a form of community cinema in the Islands in the 1970s and their experience was that *Whisky Galore!*

was a particular favourite among the Islanders. There are reports of versions of it being mounted by amateur dramatic groups and it is certainly more extensively revived than *The Maggie*. Since the 1960s it has been shown ten times at the National Film Theatre to *The Maggie*'s five and has been transmitted on television twenty-six times to the latter's ten. It has had a television film – Murray Grigor's *Distilling Whisky Galore!* – devoted to its making and the very fact that *Rockets Galore!* exists as a film (it was, of course, the last of Mackenzie's interlinked Scottish comic novels) is testimony to the resonance of its predecessor. *Rockets Galore!* was also produced by Monja Danischewsky and used many of the personnel associated with *Whisky Galore!* It does, in fact, have about it the rather perfunctory feel of a sequel and certainly (despite its more apparently politically serious subject matter) had nowhere near the critical and commercial success of *Whisky Galore!*

However, it is only in the last couple of years that *Whisky Galore!* has been accorded the ultimate accolade of visibility in a culture – being *parodied*. The television comedy programme *The Fast Show* did a brief version of *Whisky Galore!* as though by the makers of *Trainspotting*. It was called *Heroin Galore!*

Notes

INTRODUCTION

1. McArthur, 'The Cultural Necessity of a Poor Celtic Cinema'.
2. Eagleton, *The Significance of Theory*, p. 73.
3. Cited in Eagleton, *Marxism and Literary Criticism*, p. 34.

1. THE MOMENT(S) OF *WHISKY GALORE!* AND *THE MAGGIE*

1. Linklater, *Compton Mackenzie: a Life*, p. 147.
2. Jordan and Weedon, *Cultural Politics*, pp. 179–81.
3. Chapman, *The Gaelic Vision in Scottish Culture*, p. 18.
4. Danischewsky, *White Russian, Red Face*, p. 157.
5. Linklater, *Mackenzie*, p. 222.
6. Stewart, 'Out of the North Wind', p. 1068.
7. Wallace, 'Compton Mackenzie and the Scottish Popular Novel', pp. 246–7.
8. Ibid., p. 255.
9. Mackenzie, *Whisky Galore!* (1957 edn), p. 60.
10. Ibid., p. 8.
11. Ibid., p. 17.
12. Wallace, 'Compton Mackenzie and the Scottish Popular Novel', pp. 252–3.
13. Mackenzie, *Whisky Galore!*, p. 9.
14. Ibid., p. 10.
15. Ibid., p. 11.
16. Quoted in Drazin, *The Finest Years*.
17. Barr, *Ealing Studios*, p. 5.
18. Cited in ibid., p. 9.
19. Cited in ibid., p. 77.
20. Danischewsky, *White Russian*, p. 160.
21. Kemp, *Lethal Innocence*, p. 23.
22. Ibid., p. 25.
23. Forsyth, *United States Investment in Scotland*, p. 7.
24. Cited in Richards, *Films and British National Identity*, p. 192.

25. Kemp, *Lethal Innocence*, p. 89.
26. Ibid., p. 90.

2. INSIDE *WHISKY GALORE!* AND *THE MAGGIE*

1. Both quotations are from an unpublished interview with Mackendrick by Philip Kemp.
2. McArthur, *Scotch Reels*, p. 59.
3. Mackenzie, *Whisky Galore!*, p. 23.
4. Ibid., p. 23.
5. Ibid., p. 38.
6. Ibid., pp. 133–4.
7. Ibid., p. 181.
8. Kemp, *Lethal Innocence*, p. 93.
9. Cited in ibid., p. 159.
10. Cited in ibid., p. 92.
11. Cited in ibid., p. 88.
12. Wexman, *Creating the Couple*, pp. 3–4.
13. Kemp, *Lethal Innocence*, p. 103.
14. Chapman, *Gaelic Vision*, p. 82.
15. Grimble, 'Introduction' in Thomson and Grimble (eds), *The Future of the Highlands*, p. 24.

3. POST-PRODUCTION: MARKETING AND CONSUMING

1. Both quotations from a letter to the author from Michael Søby, Cultural Attaché at the Royal Danish Embassy, London.
2. Sorlin, 'From *The Third Man* to *Shakespeare in Love*'.
3. *Sight and Sound*, vol. 23, no. 4, April/June 1954, p. 199.
4. Ibid.
5. Barr, *Ealing Studios*, p. 118.
6. Ibid., p. 110.
7. Ibid., p. 115.
8. Ibid., p. 167.
9. Kemp, *Lethal Innocence*, p. xii.
10. Ibid., p. 28.
11. Ibid.
12. Ibid., p. 34.
13. Ibid.
14. Ibid., p. 89.

Sources

Balcon, Michael, *Michael Balcon Presents ... A Lifetime of Films* (London, 1969).

Barr, Charles, *Ealing Studios* (London, 1977).

Chapman, Malcolm, *The Gaelic Vision in Scottish Culture* (London, 1978).

Cook, Pam, *Fashioning the Nation: Costume and Identity in British Cinema* (London, 1996).

Danischewsky, Monja, *White Russian, Red Face* (London, 1966).

Drazin, Charles, *The Finest Years: British Cinema of the 1940s* (London, 1998).

Eagleton, Terry, *Marxism and Literary Criticism* (London, 1976).

—— *The Significance of Theory* (London, 1990).

Ellis, John, 'Made in Ealing', *Screen*, Vol. 16, no. 1, Spring 1975, pp. 78–127.

—— 'The Quality Film Adventure: British Critics and the Cinema 1942–48', in Andrew Higson (ed.), *Dissolving Views: Key Writings on British Cinema* (London, 1996), pp. 66–93.

Forsyth, David J. C., *United States Investment in Scotland* (New York, 1972).

Geraghty, Christine, *British Cinema in the Fifties: Gender, Genre and the 'New Look'* (London, 2000).

Grigor, Murray, 'Whisky Galore!', in Eddie Dick (ed.), *From Limelight to Satellite: a Scottish Film Book* (London and Glasgow, 1990), pp. 103–14.

Grimble, Ian, 'Introduction' in Derick Thomson and Ian Grimble (eds), *The Future of the Highlands* (London, 1968).

Jordan, Glenn and Chris Weedon, *Cultural Politics: Class, Gender, Race and the Postmodern World* (London, 1995).

Kemp, Philip, *Lethal Innocence: the Cinema of Alexander Mackendrick* (London, 1991).

Linklater, Andro, *Compton Mackenzie: a Life* (London, 1992).

Lovell, Alan, 'British Cinema: the Known Cinema', in Robert Murphy (ed.), *The British Cinema Book* (London, 1997), pp. 235–43.

McArthur, Colin (ed.), *Scotch Reels: Scotland in Cinema and Television* (London, 1982).

—— 'The Maggie', *Cencrastus*, no. 12, Spring 1983, pp. 10–14.

—— 'The Cultural Necessity of a Poor Celtic Cinema', in John Hill, Martin McLoone and Paul Hammond (eds), *Border Crossing: Film in Ireland, Britain and Europe* (London and Belfast, 1994), pp. 112–25.

— 'Artists and Philistines: the Irish and Scottish Film Milieux', *Journal for the Study of British Cultures*, Vol. 5, no. 2, 1998, pp. 143–53.

Mackenzie, Compton, *Whisky Galore!* (London, 1947) (page references in the endnotes are to the Reprint Society's 1951 edition).

— *My Life and Times: Octave 9, 1946–53* (London, 1970).

Petrie, Duncan, *Screening Scotland* (London, 2000).

Richards, Jeffrey, *Films and British National Identity: From Dickens to Dad's Army* (London, 1997).

Sorlin, Pierre, 'From *The Third Man* to *Shakespeare in Love*: Fifty Years of British Success on Continental Screens', in Justine Ashby and Andrew Higson (eds), *British Cinema, Past and Present* (London, 2000), pp. 80–91.

Stewart, J. L. M., 'Out of the North Wind', *Times Literary Supplement*, 9 September 1977, p. 1068.

Wallace, Gavin, 'Compton Mackenzie and the Scottish Popular Novel', in Cairns Craig (ed.), *History of Scottish Literature*, vol. 4: *Twentieth Century*, pp. 242–56.

Wexman, Virginia Wright, *Creating the Couple: Love, Marriage, and Hollywood Performance* (Princeton, NJ, 1993).

Williams, Tony, *Structures of Desire: British Cinema, 1939–1955* (New York, 2000).